"Lisa has powerfully raised a challenge that can no longer be ignored by the church. It is time for women to rise up and take their place alongside men for kingdom purposes . . . We need to celebrate and embrace differences rather than try to eliminate them. This book will help free women from the many impositions and limitations that have held them back from realizing their God-given potential. I could not put this book down."

—Chris Caine, author and director, Equip and Empower Ministries

"Lisa Bevere wants to help women reach their potential, value their role, and discover God's plan for their lives. The message she shares in this book will bring freedom and confidence, and help women of all ages take positive steps toward wholeness. I rejoiced as I read this book, realizing that it is never too late to learn to 'fight like a girl.'"

—Betty Robison, cohost, *LIFE Today*

"Through the pages of this book the question, 'Where are the fearless daughters who are ready to fight like girls?' is answered in a profound, yet simple way. Lisa challenges all the 'Deborahs' of the world to rise up, awaken to their potential, and receive the truth of God's Word. Lisa urges women to put down their carnal weapons, pick up their spiritual swords, and use them as instruments of transformation. Be prepared for the extreme makeover that is about to take place in your heart as you read this book."

—Nancy Alcorn, president and founder, Mercy Ministries of America

"Women are magnificent and Lisa has done a great job of painting that picture! This is a must-read for all of us who are on the journey to fulfill the purpose for which we were created. We are the loved daughters of the King and have a tremendous role to play here on the planet. In her own amazing style, Lisa is challenging us to love passionately, grow in strength, overcome obstacles, and recognize our own beauty. A truly powerful book. Don't just buy one . . . get one for your friend!"

—Holly Wagner, author *GodChicks* and *When It Pours, He Reigns*

Boxing Glove: Strike when the enemy draws near.
Purse: Spend your influence wisely.
Heart: You are a guardian of the heart.
Sword: Wield God's Word to elevate life.
Cross: Jesus is your ultimate love and source of life.
Stiletto Heel: The enemy is under your feet.

Fight Like *a Girl*

THE POWER OF BEING A WOMAN

Lisa Bevere

New York   Boston   Nashville

FaithWords
Hachette Book Group
237 Park Avenue
New York, NY 10017

www.faithwords.com

Scriptures are from the following sources:
The Amplified Bible, Expanded Edition (AMP): Copyright © 1987 by The Zondervan Corporation and The Lockman Foundation. All rights reserved; The Holy Bible, New Century Version® (NCV). Copyright © 1987, 1988, 1991 by Word Publishing, a Division of Thomas Nelson, Inc. Used by permission. All rights reserved; The Holy Bible, New International Version (NIV). Copyright © 1973, 1978, 1984, International Bible Society. Used by permission of Zondervan Bible Publishers; The King James Version of the Bible (KJV); The Living Bible (TLB), copyright © 1971 by Tyndale House Publishers, Wheaton, Ill. Used by permission; The New King James Version (NKJV®), copyright © 1979, 1980, 1982, Thomas Nelson, Inc., Publishers; Holy Bible, New Living Translation, copyright © 1996. Used by permission of Tyndale House Publishers, Inc., Wheaton, Illinois 60189. All rights reserved.

Printed in the United States of America

Originally published in hardcover by Hachette Book Group.

First Trade Edition: May 2008
10 9 8 7 6 5 4 3 2

FaithWords is a division of Hachette Book Group, Inc.
The FaithWords name and logo are trademarks of Hachette Book Group, Inc.

ISBN 978-0-446-69468-1 (pbk.)
LCCN: 2005937858

To my husband, John, who has always celebrated my life and passions. Thanks for encouraging me to pursue truth and to never be satisfied with anything less. I love you more than ever and thank God you are the knight in my life. To my four sons, Addison, Austin, Alec, and Arden, you inspire me more than you know. You are each a gift from heaven. May honor encompass your lives. To my sweet Viking Jacque, you and daughters like you are the reason I write. May you go further and farther and defeat the enemy at the gate. Debby, you were a constant source of support and one of my favorite people. To all the beautiful women who just want to do the woman thing well, may we fully recover all that has been lost.

Table of Contents

Fight Like *a Girl*

CHAPTER ONE

You Fight Like a Girl!

Hey, you fight like a girl! Of course, this phrase is usually meant as an insult. Whether it is spoken guy to guy, boy to girl, or woman to man, it is not meant as a compliment. No, it is hurled in response to a weak punch, a scratch, or even a cheap shot. So why would I be encouraging anyone to fight like a girl? First, an insult to men or boys should not always be heard as one by women. Girls are meant to fight like girls, but for some odd reason, most of us would rather be told we fight like men. Could this be because girls have developed the habit of fighting dirty?

Before we even start, I do not want you to think I am a girly girl advocating whipping people with frilly pink ribbons. I am not. I like to surf, ski, and hunt (in that order). I live with five men and travel internationally, more often than not, by myself. I am a cancer survivor, a mother, and a wife, but I was first a daughter. I am not advocating we dumb it down or fake something we are not. I do think we need to ask why it is an insult to fight like a girl. Even better, I want girls and women to consider themselves complimented if they are told they fight like one.

Actually, it is quite possible we've forgotten what it looks like to fight like a girl. For so long we have attempted to fight like men, and if this didn't work, we have taken some cheap shots or even cheated! Others of us have simply hidden from the storm of conflict raging around us and imagined we were being feminine and ladylike to do so. Others have forgotten that what is considered weakness in one gender is often strength in the other. I mean, should not hitting as hard as a man always be viewed as wrong?

Boys earn the respect of their peers when they fight like boys. They are considered brave and strong when they fight for what is important to males. They are admired for standing up to bullies, protecting younger children, and upholding the honor of their family name. It is when boys don't stand up for what is right that they are mocked and the name-calling begins. "Sissy!" or "Mama's boy!" might be taunts a boy will hear when he hasn't measured up to his peers' idea of a male. This dynamic doesn't change with age; men who fight and respond like women are considered weak or effeminate. Men and boys should fight with the power and strength innately entrusted to them. Men are physically stronger, and therefore have the proverbial upper hand when it comes to physical feats. This being true, what is the strength of a woman? Different issues and conflicts arouse a man's ire. What should upset a woman? And what would fighting like a girl look like if it was done right?

> *What would fighting like a girl look like if it was done right?*

Women and Battle

Before we delve deeper and answer this, perhaps you might be questioning whether women are even to be included in fights or conflict. To answer this, we need to revisit original intent or the reason behind our origin. Women were not initially formed for battle, but for life, nurture, and relationship. Perhaps this is why we often do not wear conflict well. This being true, is it wrong for women to fight? No, not any more than it is wrong for men to fight. Neither was initially created for destruction—they were both formed for increase, order, and cultivation. And the day will come when weapons will be laid aside in favor of this mandate. The Bible says swords will be beaten once again into plowshares (see Isaiah 2:4). Then both men and women will return to their original positions and relational dynamic on the earth. But right now there is a problem, an enemy, and a battle.

This ultimate responsibility and privilege were Adam's and Eve's. They were entrusted with the earth in its fullness. They had every resource necessary to create both increase and order so every living thing could flourish. With the fall of man everything changed; dominion became domination, multiplication became division, and order spiraled into chaos. Flourishing gave way to decay as fruit-bearing plants and trees wrestled thorns and thistles. Life-giving seed fought for space in soil tangled with weeds and dead underbrush. Even before this upheaval exerted itself on the earth, the last to be created became the first in conflict. The stage was set for battle.

> *And I will put enmity between you and the woman.*
>
> (Genesis 3:15 NIV)

To grasp an understanding of both the magnitude and the weight of this struggle, we must first define *enmity*. I used to substitute the word *enemy* or *hatred* when I read this passage. I mean, it's not as though we go around using the word *enmity* in everyday conversation. The problem with my substitutions was that, though similar in meaning, these words were not severe enough. Unger's Bible Dictionary defines *enmity* as both "deep-rooted hatred and irreconcilable hostility."[1] Don't confuse *enmity* with the term *irreconcilable differences* we are so accustomed to hearing cited in divorce proceedings, but rather "irreconcilable *hostilities*." This speaks of a hatred so profound, it is destined to not only exist perpetually, but to deepen and expand without end. To capture this in mathematical language, imagine a single point from which two rays or arrows emanate. One moves west, the other east. Both travel in these opposing directions without the possibility of ever meeting. These arrows do not span the curve of our globe; they travel the linear paths of time. This means the polarity of perpetual hostilities increases with the passage of time as both sides expand and multiply in reach and number. Generation after generation, the hostility deepens.

Enmity is such an intense word, it is used only eight times in the Bible. After its introduction in Genesis, enmity reaches its dark arm forward to encompass and harass the woman's seed. We see its influence extend to the book of Revelations.

> *Then the dragon became angry at the woman, and he declared war against the rest of her children—all who keep God's commandments and confess that they belong to Jesus.*
>
> (Revelation 12:17 NLT)

Who wages this never-ending war against Eve, her daughters, and every human life who passes through the womb? A serpent, the prince of the power of the air. The war started by a cunning serpent now encompasses the great dragon and all his adherents (see Genesis 3:15; John 8:44). In the garden, he skillfully wielded his weapon of deception and effectively stole the dominion of the earth from the two who were one.

To win, the enemy had to divide to conquer. He accomplished this by enlisting the support of the woman. To cause Adam to forfeit his position, he needed more than deception. Satan used the power of the woman's influence. Without her influence, it is quite possible the man might not have yielded to the serpent's counsel. He surrendered to the voice of his wife. He watched her eat, and when nothing appeared to change, he stretched forth his hand and received it from her.

She took some and ate it. She also gave some to her husband,
who was with her, and he ate it.   (Genesis 3:6 NIV)

At creation's dawn, I believe Eve's beauty and power of influence were
so profound as to quite possibly be irresistible. The perfect world with
the perfect woman contained a perfect adversary. Had Adam not been
warned to guard and keep the tree?

Why had the magnificent Eve, mother of all living, used her ability to
sway her husband to both their detriment? I believe we can assume she
did not know she was leading him astray. She obviously thought she had
counseled him well. But we are never truly wise when we move outside
God's wisdom. What had this tempter offered to get them to willingly
jeopardize so much?

When the woman saw that the fruit of the tree was good for
food and pleasing to the eye, and also desirable for gaining
wisdom . . .   (Genesis 3:6 NIV)

I am certain that many trees in this garden were good for food and
pleasant to look at. But a tree whose fruit had the power to elevate one
to the status of God was quite another thing. Eve thought there was
something more than what she had already been given. I find it amazing that the woman would grasp at something she was not to have
(equality with God), and in the process lose something she already had
(the potential to possess wisdom). In addition to this, the serpent ap-
pealed to Adam's and Eve's desire to be like God outside His sphere of
influence and authority. Both the man and the woman grasped for a
role that was not theirs to take. Ages later Eve's seed, Jesus, would re-
verse their folly.

Who, being in very nature God, did not consider equality
with God something to be grasped, . . . (Philippians 2:6 NIV)

They were in fact made in the image of God, but not equal to Him. The "image" of something speaks of a reflection, not representation in its entirety. Through his deceptive rhetoric, the serpent caused them both to think they were receiving something, when in actuality they both lost. He had not enlightened them; he darkened their understanding, but they thought it wisdom. This serpent was not looking to befriend them—he wanted them disempowered and displaced. Having been formerly stripped of his position, he needed theirs. Far too often when deception speaks, you forget both who you are and who your true allies are.

Lost Purpose, Lost Places

We frequently lose what we have because we fail to remember why it was given. Adam and Eve forgot their purpose and lost their place. They knew they were created for dominion, but they forgot why. Grasping for what was lost, they began to misuse their strengths, and used their dominion against rather than for each other. Essentially, the fall of man originated the battle of the

> *We frequently lose what we have because we fail to remember why it was given.*

sexes. Thus, the wrestling began.

Have we learned anything in all the years of pain? How many parents have lost the hearts of their children because they forgot why they had them? It was never to control them but to provide an environment in which they would flourish. How many couples have lost their marriages because they forgot why they were together? They fight against each other rather than for their love. Do we grasp and wrestle with others for their roles because we lose sight of our own? We all lose when we take from others what was not theirs to give. Why are we not content to walk in the authority and positions entrusted to our care?

The man's position is not up for grabs, just as it is not his to give away. The woman's place is not the man's for the taking, nor is it hers to forfeit. The two must stand together in their respective roles. What we have been given to guard, we should never yield to another. The man and the woman gave away what they had been entrusted to protect and steward in the Garden of Eden. We have spent all this time trying to find our way back to Eden, God's paradise, where His creation again flourishes. This once-lush garden is long gone, though the seeds of truth and principle remain. We long for the restoration of our lost paradise. It was a type and shadow of the new we will ultimately realize. In the Spirit, Jesus Christ, the seed of Eve, secured this victory for us.

> *He will crush your head, and you will strike his heel.*
>
> (Genesis 3:15 NIV)

So where is this reversal? Where is the evidence of our enemy's defeat? When will we see darkness compressed and oppression released? When will the children of Eve begin to walk out the victory won by her seed? I believe we will begin to see a turnaround as we stop misusing our power and authority. What would happen if women used their powers of insight and influence for healing and nurture? What if men used their power of might for truth and justice? What if men fought as men? What if women were truly empowered to fight like girls? We would all win.

Men would win the respect they have lost, and women would recover the power of love. Know that what has been lost is being restored. The way things are is yielding to the way it should be. Come to this place of truth with me. Women, let these words speak to you, and find yourself again released to be all you were created to be.

> *What has been lost is being restored.*

> *The Lord announces victory, and throngs of women shout the happy news. Enemy kings and their armies flee, while the women of Israel divide the plunder.* (Psalm 68:11–12 NLT)

God is declaring victory, and it is time for the daughters to joyously shout the truth of what was won. This triumph is too vast for one voice to contain. We need the voices of many who speak as one. The lie has been far-reaching, but the truth is more powerful. If we will but declare the truth, the enemy kings and armies will flee. In the wake of their departure, we will find the riches and treasures, so long lost, restored.

Totally Free, Totally God's

It is for freedom that Christ has set us free. (Galatians 5:1 NIV)

God is all about freedom. It is a very big idea for Him. He wants you totally free so you can be totally His. Over the years, I have come to believe God actually enjoys putting us in positions and situations that have the potential to really challenge areas of bondage in our lives. I think He enjoys watching His children pushed into realms outside their comfort and control. Perhaps from His perspective, it is no different from when I watch my children flip and dance among the waves.

It is important that you understand I used to be basically a very fearful person. Even writing a book that suggested conflict would have scared me. But then the time came when my desire to be safe was exceeded by my desire to be free. Are we there yet? For me this happened when I saw my fears echoed in my children. If it had just been about me, I honestly don't know if I would have changed. It would have been easier in a lot of ways if I had stayed hidden.

Case in point: In high school, I was required to take either speech or debate to graduate. No prospect could have frightened me more. I was terrified of getting up in front of people. I had lost an eye to a form of cancer called retinoblastoma when I was five years old.

Overnight, life as I'd known it changed. I went from being confident and outgoing to being sullen and withdrawn. I felt that people no longer saw me. I watched as they tried to determine which eye they should look at when they spoke to me. At school, compliments changed to name-calling. I was dubbed "One Eye" and "Cyclops." I put up a tough front in an attempt to act as though their words didn't hurt. I'd ignore the comments and just maintain my composure until I made it home; then I'd cry inconsolably in my room. Why couldn't I be like everyone else?

Now I was going to have to get up in front of my classmates and give a speech. Debate was not an option. There was no way I could even imagine winning an argument in front of others. I endured the first few weeks of class; then it was time for the speeches. I prepared, but it didn't matter. When the day came I couldn't speak. The teacher gave me an opportunity to walk out of the classroom and start again, but I couldn't. I looked at my classmates, and nothing would come out. I excused myself and ran down to the guidance counselor's office. I explained how it was impossible for me to successfully complete a speech class. How could I get a C, let alone an A or a B? I was handicapped, after all! My counselor was surprisingly sympathetic. He asked a few questions, including, "Are you planning to do anything with your life that requires public speaking?" Absolutely not! I assured him I had no intention of speaking in front of more than two people for the rest of my life.

"I'll tell you what, just pick another unit of languages arts, and we will waive the requirement for speech." I couldn't believe my ears.

Right then and there, I signed up for a course on Kurt Vonnegut.

Since the counselor was so understanding, I brought another class to his attention that was a major problem for me—typing. It was nearly impossible for me to go above twenty-five words per minute. He listened patiently as I made the case.

"I suppose we can waive typing as well. You can always pay someone to type your papers in college."

I was elated! I left feeling as if a giant weight had been lifted from my shoulders. I gathered my stuff from the speech classroom and presented the note to my new teacher, alerting him I would be joining the Vonnegut class. Typing turned into study hall. Life was good. But God in heaven must have been laughing. I can just imagine Him turning to the angels and saying, "Poor Lisa. Let's give her a break. I understand she's too frightened to get up in front of twelve classmates. We'll just wait and really scare her and make it hundreds then thousands and throw TV in the mix just to push her totally over the edge. She doesn't want to type. It's too hard for her. Okay, she might as well rest now, because she'll be typing for the rest of her life."

The two classes I got out of in high school are what I do on a regular basis today. You see, counselors, teachers, and various organizations may all agree with you that you are handicapped, but God never will.

He loves giving you the opportunity to face what you fear, because when you face what you fear you become fearless.

Where are the fearless daughters who are ready to fight like girls?

As you turn these pages, open your heart. Believe you are one of these voices, one of those daughters of the Most High God who will learn how to fight like a girl. It is time to take it all back from the serpent, put on our high heels, and crush his head.

Heavenly Father,

I come before You in the name of Jesus. I believe You see me as lovely. I believe You created me and knit me in my mother's womb for good and not for harm. I have been attacked as a problem; I want to be released as an answer. I lift my face to You; restore the tenderness of my voice. I want to bring healing and hope to a lost and dying world, but first

I need You to intimately touch and heal my own life. Change my perspective. Restore my soul. Call me lovely. Hold me close. I remove the awkward costume and come before You ready to be redressed in the splendor of my origin. Spirit, breathe life on every dead and barren place. Open my eyes to see what can be, and open my ears to hear You call me by name. Amen.

CHAPTER TWO

What if I Don't Like Women?

This is what I used to say. The truth is, now I love women. As you can surely imagine, there was a time when I was not particularly fond of them. Not only did I not like women, I resented being one. Therefore, I was not surprised by the concert of anti-female sentiment from my fellow sisters. I have heard one form or another of this sentiment expressed by women of all ages and walks of life. Actually, as I travel and speak, it has become a major connection point. I will open my session by saying something like,

"How many of you in here today aren't sure you like women?"

"I mean, honestly, I think I am more male than female."

"I like the guys so much better than girls."

"The men say what they mean and mean what they say. With women, you never know where you stand!"

"I get along better with guys; female relationships take way too much energy!"

"Women are petty gossips who say one thing to your face and another behind your back."

I'm fairly certain I have either publicly or privately expressed all these sentiments and frustrations. But when I really think about this dynamic, it is a bit frightening. Let's dress it up a bit differently. I cannot even imagine a group of men affirming another brother as he openly declares his disdain for the male populace. Or how about a black brother or sister getting up and announcing to their community, "Hey, folks, you know what? I really don't like black people." It's just not going to go over well. Extend this to any people group—Italians, Arabs, children, etc.—and it sounds equally strange. It is just not going to fly except with women.

Why are the majority of women in agreement with their general disgust and frustration with females? I've even seen it celebrated: "You don't like women? Great, neither do I!" As if this should make us all feel somehow safe that we are surrounded by women who don't like women. Granted, we usually like the individual women present, but we wrestle with the concept of women as a whole. As the conversation progresses, we will further position our allegiances by going around the table and affirming our masculine approach to life and relationships.

"Women are so emotional!"
"They're a bunch of whiners!"
"They're so passive-aggressive!"
"You just can't trust them!"

I have repeatedly said I'd rather navigate conversations in a room full of men than talk shop with a handful of women. This is tragic, but far too often true.

What's Wrong with Women?

I think this epidemic of anti-female sentiment needs some explanation, and we might best begin by answering the question "Why is it that women don't like women?" What could possibly cause a large portion of the female populace to reject their own gender? I have seen this everywhere I travel, and the fallout is huge. Unfortunately, many of us have not been taught an appreciation for who we are as women. Is it so surprising, then, that we would distance ourselves from the role if we've never possessed a true understanding of what it is to be a woman?

This lack of awareness of feminine value needs to be confronted in almost every realm of life if we are to see a turnaround. God is awakening our individuality to enable us to realize what we can become as daughters, wives, mothers, sisters, leaders, and friends. Women have significant contributions to make to their unique spheres of influence, and these will never fully be realized with an underlying distaste for our gender.

I vividly remember an incident that happened shortly after John and I were engaged. We were sitting in a park, discussing the future of our life together, when I had a complete meltdown. The realization had come crashing down on me: *I was a female.* The pending prospect of our marriage was making it very apparent. I

> *I had blurted out, "I hate being a girl!"*

would be playing the feminine role for the rest of my life. John was overjoyed as he pictured our future stretching out before him, but as he spoke, I began to panic. Before I knew what I was doing I had blurted out, "I hate being a girl!"

John was stunned. What exactly was his bride-to-be saying? Then I burst into tears (my embarrassing response to frustration) as I elaborated on just how awful and limiting it was to be a female. I was afraid that by agreeing to marriage I was forfeiting control over my life, and signing up for much more than I'd bargained for. After a nearly fifteen-minute dissertation, it was John's turn to be afraid. Thankfully, we were in the neighborhood of a godly couple who were like parents to John. He thought it might be a good idea for us to take a walk and drop by their place, so I could debrief with the wife. John had tried his best, but once worked up, I was not easily consoled.

We were warmly welcomed and invited in by this lovely woman. I slipped in and headed straight for the guest bath to compose myself. While I was out of the room, John felt the need to offer an explanation for my disheveled look and tear-streaked face.

"Lisa just said she wishes she were a man and that she hates being a woman," he offered, unsure of her reaction. The wise woman nodded, reserving comment until I had returned. I came out a bit sheepish. What would she think of my silly outburst? Had she warned John, "Don't marry her!"? Almost immediately, she set my fears to rest. She drew me near, looked me in the eyes, and simply said, "I understand." I took a deep breath and regrouped. For the time, it seemed enough to simply be understood by another woman who was older and wiser.

It is probably more accurate to say it isn't really that we don't like women; rather, we just don't like the image women have evolved or adapted to represent. At other times I have to wonder if there is something crucial missing; that we mourn the loss of that to which we no longer give expression. Perhaps we don't like the perceived limitations or weaknesses associated with our gender. Just look at how the media exploit women and simultaneously dishonor men. We claim equal value, then allow ourselves to be reduced to mere sexual expressions toying with others. Somehow we appear to have lost our way, and quite a few of us are desperately attempting to navigate some of these truths rather late in the game of life. I fear it is imperative we regain our bearings before it is too late.

A Vision to Inspire Us

I can't even count the number of times I have had earnest young women ask me thought-provoking, probing questions. Why is it good to be a woman? Where is our value? What is our role? What can I do? How can I do it? What does God say about our feminine expression? Can my life truly have meaning outside a relationship with a man? I sense God's calling, but I don't know what that looks like as a woman. Can you tell me how to be that woman?

To successfully review and examine your feminine destiny (and yes, it really is that powerful), allow me to lend you both perspective and desire.

Imagine, if you will, a magnificent city. It is no ordinary place, for it appears only at dawn where the earth meets the sky, as though born with the rising sun. You see its outline etched against a fiery coral glow each morning, so real, so right, you feel you could pluck it from the horizon and hold it in your hand. Then suddenly it is gone, for as the sun climbs, this mythical city disappears from sight.

You have been told that though the city is real, it is distant. The inhabitants of this city are very different from us, for all are strong, beautiful, good, and wise. The city's culture and customs are completely foreign to our own. The gates are always open, and legend says those who enter the city rarely desire to leave. The kingdom lavishes gifts on all who come, yet its spacious borders are never filled. There is room for all. But all do not make room for this place.

Sadly, most are not willing to journey to a land they glimpse only on clear mornings. Those who do journey to this realm rarely return.

Each day your thoughts turn to the city, but other activities and things vie for your attention. Thoughts and worries crowd your mind and effectively distract you. Conflicting messages fight against the city's pristine beauty. Yet when you are quiet you feel irresistibly drawn, as though summoned. At times you awake and catch a whisper. You hear your name, but it sounds somehow different . . . it resonates with life. It is as though now only a small portion of your identity is realized, but there you would be complete. Some may think I describe only heaven—I do not. I speak of embracing now the promises and truth of a coming kingdom.

> *Thy Kingdom come. Thy will be done on earth, as it is in heaven.*   (Matthew 6:10 KJV)

I believe as the truth of heaven's kingdom is not only heard but also passionately lived, we will see a portion of our power and beauty restored. This city speaks of the way things should be and are not. It represents a culture where all have unique value and honor. It is the difference between a lofty heaven and our present earth. This vast expanse communicates both destiny and longing. I believe vision is a powerful agent for awakening destiny.

> *Where there is no vision, the people perish.*
> (Proverbs 29:18 KJV)

Yes, vision has the power to lift and remind us we're ultimately fashioned for another place and time. There, all wrongs will be made right, and we will discover we are altogether lovely. It is our hope, but what about now?

Splendor: A Woman's Gift

Earlier this year, I actually felt as though a vision danced before me. I was in Australia at a wonderful women's conference. At the close of the event, a group of teenage girls performed a beautiful dance. I was captivated as I watched them assemble. They were of all shapes and sizes— tall, short, curvaceous, and slender—yet when the music began they moved with a common grace. Both the song and the dance fit them all. Tears traced my cheeks as they wove a tapestry of elegance. One brunette repeatedly caught my eye. I thought to myself, *Isn't she lovely?*

No sooner was this thought present than I heard the Spirit whisper, *That is what you looked like at her age, but you never saw it.* I looked again. Her frame did mirror mine at her age, yet I'd always seen myself as ugly and awkward. Why did I see it so differently now? I looked over at my dear friend Leigh, who sat next to me, and smiled. Her eyes brimmed with tears as well. It was different now. We were mothers watching daughters dance.

It is amazing what time and a change of perspective can do. As the years have passed, I no longer feel pressure to compare myself with other women. God has healed those broken places. I am looking for something more. I am searching for what I glimpsed that day. I long for the day when daughters will begin to weave this garment and restore the unique splendor, love, and beauty that only the expression of the feminine brings. I am watching for women who know how to adorn not only their lives but also the lives of others with a portion of heaven's splendor. That moment captures what I want this book to do. I want the daughters to dance unafraid while mothers smile and grandmothers sigh with contentment.

I want to be the voice of a mother to the young, a friend to my sisters, and a daughter to those who now rest awhile after so many years of dancing. I want to help women capture the beauty and strength of their life seasons. No matter what our present season or perspective, this cannot happen until we first learn to love one another and who we are as women.

Breaking Through the Static

I do not have all the answers, but what I have learned I am willing to share. There were many times when truth spoke to me, but I did not listen. Often it called to me, but I did not hear it. I was too busy listening to lies. Unfortunately, if you listen to lies long enough, when truth speaks you cannot hear or bear it. At other times, I didn't understand what was spoken because of all the interference and static in my life.

For years I have heard many different and mixed messages about women. When I was younger I heard feminist leaders speak, but then there was always the static of their anger. As I grew I heard the voices of divorced women, and there was the noise of their disappointment, hurt, bitterness, and betrayal. In college I heard the philosophy of my sociology instructor, but there was the interference of her agenda. In church I heard the views of leaders, and frequently there was the static of religious systems. Each voice carried a portion of truth. These were true stories of hardship and injustice, of domination and loss. When I put these pieces together, I did not like the resulting picture or the options it presented me. I wanted something more. I wanted the dance. I wanted to smile. I wanted the city on the horizon.

As we journey toward the way things should be, each of us will travel from different places or perspectives, but it is imperative as women that we get there. It is my earnest prayer that we will span this distance and in the process create a bridge for daughters young and old to traverse. And so our quest toward truth begins.

In order to find our way, we must first turn off the ever-present static, for it dangerously muffles and distorts all we hear. This interference had become a constant in my life. I even heard its persistent distortion as I read the Scriptures. I heard it in marriage relational dynamics. I heard it in sitcoms. I heard it in policies and procedures. I heard it in humor. I heard it in church. I heard it in school. What did the static say?

"Women are a problem."

Have you ever heard this static? Notice I did not say women can *cause* problems, because surely they can, but women *are* a problem. It is one thing to be a catalyst, but quite another for something negative to be inherent to or associated with your gender. Thankfully, over the years I have discovered that for every lie, there is an overriding truth: *Women are not a problem . . . they are an answer.*

> *Women are not a problem . . . they are an answer.*

Ponder this a moment. Allow the beauty and power of it to supersede the noise and penetrate your being. As you read on, you will need to repeatedly process everything you hear through this simple yet profound realization: *You are an answer.*

Embrace Your Power

"No," you may say, "I am not. I am a problem. You don't know what my life has been like." Quiet, listen, I am not speaking to your past; I am speaking to your future. If you believe you are an answer, you'll approach life and relationships in an entirely different manner than if you believe you are a problem. Problems are negative, critical, and judgmental. Problems nag your life with their worries and fears. Oh, but solutions sound and feel very different. They are positive, hopeful, and life-giving in their wisdom. Answers comfort and slay fear with the power of love. If you believe you are a problem, sooner or later you will begin to act like one. Likewise, if you believe you are not intrinsically a problem but a solution, you will begin to act like one. Imagine what might happen if a whole generation of women got this. If they looked in the mirror each day and said, "I am an answer. I have the power to rock this world. I was created for good and not harm. I don't need to roar, for I hold the power of the whisper. I don't have to be black or white . . . for I am the color and beauty of creation!"

An answer was the very reason for our existence and the motivation behind our creation. Paradise had a problem, and we were God's answer. Think of it! You are somebody's answer. You are something's answer. There is a problem out there only your presence can solve. There is a broken and wounded heart to which only you can administer healing. You are a voice to the mute. You are beauty amid desolation. You are not a victim; you are an answer. Imagine the power in this change of perspective. Women are not men, but they are often the men's answer.

> *It is not good for the man to be alone. I will make a compan-*
> *ion who will help him.*   (Genesis 2:18 NLT)

Adam needed help. Eve was his answer. Answers or solutions don't have to fight to make their presence known when they come on the scene. The wise know this. Adam sure did.

> *"At last!" Adam exclaimed. "She is part of my own flesh and*
> *bone! She will be called 'woman,' because she was taken out*
> *of a man."*   (Genesis 2:23 NLT)

Just as with Adam, when people see women begin to embody truth, they will leave the problem mind-set and embrace the role of an answer. I believe there is a world out there watching and waiting for you to be an answer.

Granted, we live in a world and often in a church culture that repeat-edly communicates that women are a bit of a "wrench in the engine." A weak link, so to speak. Oh, but this is just not true!

Woman was made to be an answer. She was the treasure for whom Adam searched—God's perfect creation. When she loves she is the oil that anoints and makes life run smoothly. When she is free she is not the weakest link; she is the ruby pendant suspended by a length of gold.

> *Let me see your face, let me hear your voice; for your voice is*
> *sweet, and your face is lovely.*   (Song of Solomon 2:14 NKJV)

There is a world that longs to see and hear you. The daughters of Eve have foolishly believed a lie and allowed it to change their perspective and image. By embracing the lie that we were a problem, as time passed we became one. By forgetting we were lovely, we lost a portion of our beauty. It is true that most of us don't disappoint those who watch for our failure. But the wind is shifting, and truth is blowing free and fresh to all who have ears to hear what truth would speak and awaken. The world longs to hear the loveliness of our voices again.

Women Aren't the Problem

It's not that you don't like women . . . you don't like the dance we are now doing. The costume is uncomfortable and the song is awkward. You have sought to distance yourself from shallowness, frailties, and failings, and this is not actually a bad thing. But it is not enough. Denying our gender will never move us from the problem dynamic to the answer.

I, too, have judged myself simply for being female. My self-talk went something like this: "I hate it that I'm a girl . . . I wish I were a guy! Guys are free to do so much more. Darn it, they are stronger. I hate being dominated and submitting! I want to be free to boss myself." As time has passed, I've realized these thoughts were all formed in response to the static. Noise distorted my interpretation of everything.

Think of this process as similar to a GPS system in a car. The mapping satellite has the benefit of a perspective far above the tangle of traffic or interior car distractions (such as loud children). My husband has such a system in his car, and one time I attempted to use it when I ventured into an unfamiliar portion of Denver. The only problem was that it had been programmed incorrectly; it had my point of departure as my destination.

For the whole trip, the navigation system was trying to bring me back home. Exit immediately and turn back! Take the next exit. Stop, you're heading the wrong way! Having said all this, sometimes I have felt my approach to gender issues was the same. I had unwittingly been programmed with the wrong goal. Destination: Male Boulevard, leaving Female Freeway. Perhaps you feel this way as well; your navigation system is screaming, but you don't know where to turn. It is time for us to exit this high-speed mixed-up highway and go back to a safe road that takes us to the kingdom on the horizon. There we can celebrate not only women as friends, but grow into so much more than we ever dreamed.

Vital to God's Plan

Don't imagine I am advocating surrender or a doormat mentality. You are a vital part of God's answer for humanity. Our heavenly Father has specifically formed you to do a task no other woman can accomplish in our space and time. As I continue to address women and the issues they face, I hope to bond with my audiences by saying what God says about them: "I like women; they are an answer to so many problems."

Women are incredibly valuable, but often we have failed to express this to one another. Perhaps we have not heard it enough. Not in the media. Not in the church. Not in our homes. Not in the area of sexuality. Not in our relationships. As we realize and affirm our inherent value, our strengths will be magnified. What we will become will be increasingly apparent. The dark, shadowy mirror will clear, and our original role and the beauty it carries will be revealed.

> *Now we see but a poor reflection as in a mirror; then we shall see face to face.*　　　　(1 Corinthians 13:12 NIV)

In the pages to come, we will explore what this looks like. I pray you will find your niche in the kingdom and begin to hear Him call you by name.

Following are some questions for you to ponder:

In what ways do you allow the static to convince you that you are a problem?

At what age do you think you became most vulnerable to the interference?

Why did you start believing it?

What has happened in your life to reinforce this distortion?

What are the areas in which the image of yourself as a problem most strongly rises against you?

What must you do to believe you are an answer?

What are some areas where you can begin to be an answer to others?

CHAPTER THREE

But I Am Not a Man

As time passes, gender dynamics will become increasingly key and important. I have heard gender discrimination cited as the last prejudice to be addressed, but I feel we err to describe gender as an issue of prejudice. It is an issue of life and death. In saying this, I am in no way negating the importance of addressing oppression and prejudice in their many forms. Truly, racial prejudice continues to wreak havoc through the ignorant and arrogant in our modern world. There are many excellent resources, organizations, and individuals confronting these issues and lies. My goal is to bring healing to the existing breach between the sexes, which permeates every culture and has existed in one form or another since the dawn of time. Perhaps with the healing of the sexes, we will find healing in these other areas as well.

Race and ethnicity allow us the opportunity to celebrate the variety and diversity of every culture and nationality. God loves this vast array of expressions that highlight the facets of our humanity. Someday, each and every culture will assemble before Him and present their music, dance, and unique talents for His glory. When God the Father speaks of the man and the woman, it is a bit different. He celebrates not their division, but their union. He calls the two to become one.

This mandate can be traced back to the original garden intent, whereas ethnicity or race evolved after the Fall and our departure from the garden. Perhaps all the different flavors of the diverse cultures evolved in response to life outside the garden. But gender has always been. Gender was one of God's creative ways of expressing diversity within unity. It is the vantage that anchors our position and perspective.

For years, our culture has tried to minimize or even deny the existence of gender and the power it exerts on so many facets of life. Could this be why we have lost so much of our former strength and core bearings? Is this the kink that has left our nations, cultures, churches, families, children, and marriages with a distinct and serious wobble? History has repeatedly shown without question that whenever women are not valued, loved, and honored, there is evident or at least pending cultural collapse.

We Are Not Enemies

Men and women the world over are desperate for wholeness and healing. For far too long, pain has been the portion of both genders. Because gender issues have repeatedly been a source of injury, we have mistakenly attempted to bring about healing by blending the man and the woman. The theory was that if the differences brought wounding, perhaps their minimization would effect a cure. If somehow androgyny in the strengths resident in both sexes could be achieved, then gender would be rendered meaningless and thereby categorized as harmless. The hope was good, but the answer was inadequate. We will never find the cure we seek in this hybrid . . . we need something separate but one. The mixing of two extremes does not bring clarity, just as the mixing of black and white yields gray and indistinct hues. No, the answer we pursue will come in the form of a truer, purer seed of noble origin; and once truth is planted, I believe we will begin to see it bring forth generations of fruit.

Have we come so far yet learned so little? The difference in the human sexes is a dynamic that lends strength to both the man and the woman.

> *It is* not good *for the woman to remain hidden within the image of the man.*

This diversity was not for bad; it was for good. At the genesis of life, this was understood. It was God Himself who declared it *not good* for His glorious man Adam to be alone. Likewise, it is *not good* for the woman to remain hidden within the image of the man. The time has come for woman to be released so she can contribute her unique gifts and talents. Eve was a necessary addition to creation. Without her, the feminine image of woman could not come forth. The answer of woman cannot gain expression when she remains in hiding.

God knew this before Adam did (see Genesis 2:18, 20). He allowed the longing for a companion to work itself into Adam's being as he ordered and named creation. Perhaps God declared it *not good,* then commissioned Adam to make it *good* by ordering and designating creation in a search for what was missing.

Imagine looking for what you'd never seen. How would you recognize what had never existed? You would not know what you needed, because you would have never seen or experienced it. For Adam, there was just an innate knowing that all was not complete. No words existed to describe woman's absence; no picture or image defined her form; no sound or song of love had yet been voiced. Only lingering absence confronted Adam as he searched creation for one like him.

Though separate, the two would be complementary. Each reflected the other's absence or lack as fulfilled strength. Together, they would be joined and whole.

Imagine his joy when Eve was brought to him. She was the beautiful reflection of all he lacked. Eve was Adam's strength made perfect in weakness, for both supplied the power lacking in the other. The one (Adam) became two (Adam and Eve) so the two could again become one (in their seed). Even so, today women are the reflective complement of men in every realm of life. And their contribution has the potential to elevate every aspect they touch.

If the man alone was better than the two with separate expression, the woman would never had been created. She would have remained a rib within, hidden and expressed only in the form of secret longing. All this being true, what has happened? How did it all go so wrong?

God's Image Skewed

Are we not the ones who've allowed this image of male and female strong and united to be twisted into an unrecognizable version of its former beauty and strength? The blame for this loss is far-reaching: Our culture is at fault, our fears have driven us apart, the meanest of religions have accused us, the media have enticed us—but all these symptoms stem from a deeper, darker struggle.

We are enmeshed in a timeless battle for truth and, ultimately, power. The lies and innuendos of an ancient enemy have woven themselves into the fabric of our being and impressed themselves on every facet of our culture. Women, understand that it was not a man but a serpent that trespassed our lives and robbed us. By way of cunning and deception he stripped us of our beauty, dominion, and power. With the Fall, our vision was darkened. In the dark, it is easy to mistake enemies for friends and friends for enemies. In the realm of shadow, we often perceive differences as threats. Men and women have wrestled each other for far too long, and the time of awakening is at hand. We are not enemies . . . we are beloved allies.

Confused by past issues of pain, our culture has encouraged men to get in touch with their feminine side. While this is happening, women are coached to be more aggressive and masculine in their approach to life. Men are repeatedly asked to be *more* vulnerable or defenseless, while women have been persuaded to harden themselves. I cannot deny there exists another extreme as well. Confused religions encourage women to be stripped of all sense of self and worth and lose their identity again to the man. To our shame, far too often even evangelical churches have failed to establish healthy dynamics or parameters for men, women, and families to function and interact within.

For the woman to be lost again inside the man is both unhealthy and impossible. To actually accomplish this, the man's side would need to be reopened and the woman reinserted. How absurd! Adam's side was opened and the woman Eve was created, just as the side of Jesus the Christ was opened and His church was brought forth. The day will come when Christ and His bride will be united and one again. Now is the time for those who exemplify this relationship (the man and the woman) to be one in a healthy way. (See Ephesians 5:32.)

Stopping the Game

If we would momentarily disengage ourselves from all the cultural noise, we would be able to step back and recognize there is something terribly amiss. There appears to be some attempt at evening the sides and leveling the playing field in preparation for a giant "boys"-against-"girls" game.

The sad truth is, this type of mentality handicaps both sides in its attempt to make everything even and fair. By moving both sides toward the center, each loses their unique positions of power and strength and approaches an uncertain shade of gray. When this happens, everyone underperforms, and no one is truly challenged to grow. And who is refereeing this game, anyway? Who is it that will declare the winner? I fear it is the enemy, who has set up this game, and from it, no winner will emerge.

> *We were meant to do the dance of life together!*

The whole concept of evening the sides is wrong to start with because men and women were never meant to play or perform on opposing sides. We were meant to do the dance of life together! God never desired that men be pitted against women or women against men. Actually, the earth quakes and trembles before this folly. His plan from the very beginning was to make them joint heirs and united guardians, never divided opponents.

The Growth of Gender Distrust

In response to the overarching hurt women have experienced, many solutions have presented themselves. Years ago, feminists sought to reconcile gender inconsistencies. But what began as an attempt to right inequitable promotion, pay, and wage scales has morphed into an animal of a very different kind. No longer is it about equal pay for equal work; it has become an all-out drive to displace men. Women are insistently encouraged toward the adoption of what were previously labeled dominant male chauvinist attitudes and behavior patterns. Women are encouraged to leave their families in divorce, drop off their children for others to tend, and embrace sexuality in every form. Abortion is celebrated as independence! We should beat the men at their own game and prove ourselves their superiors. Then nothing would keep women from achieving their independence from men.

Feminists hoped these tactics would secure women positions of strength on every front: sexually, professionally, and relationally. For years, everything uniquely feminine was caricatured and relegated to women who were weak, uneducated, or lacking in valuable and/or marketable skills. These were the women who apparently could not hold a job or think for themselves. In the early 1970s, hostilities flared as the original Stepford Wives imagery assaulted the nation's psyche. I remember watching the movie as a young teen, and I found its story profoundly disturbing. Could husbands and fathers be trusted? Were all women at risk? I began to wonder, did men truly want to kill their wives and replace them with completely compliant robotic sex slaves? Was the world really supposed to revolve around men?

Advertising and articles everywhere reinforced this message of gender distrust. Overnight, the idea of loving one man completely and with abandonment became a dangerous concept. Not only would it be foolish, it would ultimately leave you unprotected. Staying home with children was akin to professional suicide, and pregnancy had the potential to enslave you to your offspring. In addition, you were thought dull and boring if you chose to stay home. How could you possibly be as exciting as the women at the office? It was implied that women were being cheated of their due "out there" if they were being provided for to stay home and nurture children. Women were roaring everywhere! This resulted in an entire generation of women who were not only afraid to trust men, but who also feared being women.

Redefining "Female"

I am the first to acknowledge there is just cause for some of these fears. Women are vulnerable when both the church and society choose not to value marriage vows. Why would women feel free to trust their husbands if life commitments were merely words? When divorce is rampant, it is always the women and children who are at the greatest risk. It is predominantly the woman who is left to care for the children with limited funds and options. But we will not find answers or safety by morphing into some type of male-female.

Our definition or image of being female should not be passed again through the parameters of man. Adam was not involved in Eve's creation; he was asleep. He gave raw material but no design or other input. However, God had his unanswered longing with which to work. Adam was not looking for a replica of himself . . . he was looking for something more. Adam was not looking for someone he could rule. He was already master of all he surveyed. He wanted someone to celebrate and share his domain with him. A wise and tender confidante who would love and admire him. Someone who would flourish under his love and care and therefore share his joy. He wanted a complementary other to do life with. He was looking for the queen of his garden.

Therefore, women acting like men could never possibly right these wrongs. Nor will we find our answers by attempting to reengineer or abandon the female gender. *We cannot become what we were created to be until we remember who we are.* The adjustments we so desperately need will come from something subtler but no less profound: I believe there must again be a revelation of woman.

No longer will we look for this daughter on a typically male playing field. In the past, women have been encouraged to prove themselves by fighting, seducing, or displacing the men to recapture a portion of their strength; but *making men look weak has never made us look strong.* No, this revelation and restoration can take place only as we return and rebuild the positions of authority and power already given to the woman by birthright.

Gender Is Everything

If there were in fact nothing a man could do that a woman could not do, and nothing a woman could do that a man could not do, then I would embrace the concept that gender was unnecessary. But this is more than simply skewed; it is a lie. For just as with the issue of timing, there are dynamics and scenarios in life where gender is everything.

Enter, if you will, into just such a scene. Envision a cold, gray dawn on a battlefield, bloody and desolate. The ground is littered with the dead and dying. In the midst of this hopeless chaos, there stands a royal daughter. She does not immediately appear out of place, for she has slipped into battle disguised in the armor of a knight. She hoped to somehow make some small contribution, even if it meant only comforting any fallen loved ones. She watched helplessly as her royal guardian was struck down and mortally wounded. She moves toward him, hoping to hold him in her arms as he slips from this earthly life. But before she can reach him, she discovers herself in the midst of an unavoidable confrontation.

Positioned in her path is an enemy so terrifying, both he and the wretched beast he rides defy human description. The beast has come to devour her wounded father. Bravely, she commands the specter and his foul dragon to leave. In response, the evil lord threatens her with endless torment if she does not yield. She refuses to give ground and draws her sword, vowing to do all within her power to hinder the fiends before her. The lord of darkness laughs, mocking her bold stance:

"Thou fool. No living man may hinder me!"

"But no living man am I! You look upon a woman . . . I am . . . a daughter. You stand between me and my lord and kin . . . I will smite you, if you touch him."

So he might see that what she speaks is true, she removes the cover of her helmet and allows her golden hair to fall free. Yes, it is a woman who stands before this dark lord, unyielding and armed with sword and shield.

> *Her eyes . . . were hard . . . yet tears were on her cheek.*
> *Suddenly the great beast . . . leaped into the air,*
> *Still she did not blanch: A swift stroke she dealt, skilled*
> *and deadly. The outstretched neck she clove asunder . . . A*
> *light fell about her, and her hair shone in the sunrise.*[1]

This royal daughter defeated the wretched enemy *no living man* could destroy. Blinded by arrogance, this dark lord was caught unaware by a feminine form on the battlefield. I am certain he did not know what had been prophesied so many ages ago . . . that evil would be at odds with the woman.

> *And I will put enmity between you and the woman.*
>   (Genesis 3:15 NIV)

I find it amazing that though she slipped into battle disguised as a man, a victory for all came when she revealed herself a woman. This is just as God intended it to be from the beginning; there is power for all with the revelation of the woman.

Then why are we so afraid to reveal ourselves as such? Why have we doubted this truth and cloaked ourselves in the armor of men? Why have we adopted Adam's voice and swagger? What drives us to fight in this awkward guise when all too frequently we lose our truer selves in its trappings?

Is it because even now a battle rages against us? Yes, there is a dark lord who seeks to destroy the woman and her children. He schemes to separate her from the love, comfort, and protection of her Lord. But what is it about the image of a woman that frightens and angers him so? For truly he would not pour so much effort into distorting and destroying something he did not fear.

The Strength of a Woman

It was years ago when I first read Tolkien's *The Return of the King* and found myself moved beyond all natural reason by its intense imagery and poetic words. I was captivated by this daughter's resolve in the face of utter hopelessness and despair. When all seemed lost, something dormant in her soul was awakened, and strength was quickened within. I loved this woman who was willing to stand her ground in the face of unspeakable terror and there reveal her womanhood. She did it all for the sake of her lord, honor, and family.

I saw a woman so determined, she would slip into a battle uninvited and fight to protect what she loved but could not hold back. I loved the imagery of eyes that were fixed, though tears streaked her face. I found a daughter who had disguised herself as a man only to find her victory as a woman. When attacked she did not cower or draw back, but remained steadfast and held her ground until the enemy came near enough for her to strike.

In that moment I was there with her. I began to weep, and my hands trembled as I laid the book aside. I sensed God's holy presence as it filled my bedroom. *What is happening?* I wondered. It was then I heard the voice of the Holy Spirit speak. I do not believe His words or the commission I received were for my ears alone. I believe it is for every daughter of the Most High with ears to hear.

> *For you truly are not a man, and there are yet battles in the spirit for the sons to fight, and there are yet battles in the spirit for the daughters to fight. Begin to call forth the daughters; cry out for them now. Call the daughters to wage the wars only they can win, and to fight the battles as only my daughters can, because truly the enemy fears this revelation more than he fears any woman who fights like a man.*

As the years have passed, this passion has grown. It is more than a passing inspiration drawn from fiction. I believe this scene somehow captured the imagery and protocol of royal daughters in battle. Women in battle are a rare and unusual phenomenon, one God reserves for only the most desperate of times. On the battlefield they do not come to fight as men, but as women.

Yet, how much more desperate can our time become? How much nearer must our enemy be before we realize it is our time to strike? Are not the daughters of God mocked and challenged on every side? How many of us have slipped into battle disguised as men, only to realize our truest form of power does not lie in forfeiting our womanhood? We are not men, and maintaining this façade hinders the revelation of our truer purpose and destiny. How can we expect the world to see the revelation of daughters when we have chosen to behave as sons?

It has become my cry, desire, and earnest prayer to see the daughters of God empowered to fight their truest enemy in their mightiest form. I long to see the daughters unsheathe the sword of God's living Word and wield it to recover what's been lost. Ancient truths were given to the daughters to both steward and reveal. It is time to shake ourselves loose of these earthly shrouds of gender fear and confusion and begin to fight for truth, honor, and our kin.

Before we move on to the next chapter, let's answer some questions:

In what areas of life have you slipped onto the battlefield disguised as a man?

Why did you take on this façade?

Why do you think women are afraid to reveal themselves?

Why have we become masters of disguise?

———————

Dear Heavenly Father,

I want to walk in truth and light. I want to reveal myself a woman. Forgive me for hiding behind the façade of a man. I believe there is ultimately more power in my revelation as a woman. Holy Spirit, have your way in my life. I want to fight in my battles in my mightiest form. I will not draw back in fear but I will boldly stake my claim to fight all that comes between my honor, my Lord and my family. Amen.

———————

CHAPTER FOUR

Finding Center

Do you sense it? Everything around us is shifting. A deep and profound unsettling is going on. Life as we know it is evolving and changing
at an extremely escalated rate.

I would not describe this change as an evolution, because this would
mean we were advancing and becoming more compatible and comfortable with our present environment. I don't feel we are moving forward. I
fear we're falling behind. There appears to be a heightened hostility between the earth and its inhabitants.

Nor do I feel "revolution" accurately describes the tumult we're
presently experiencing. There has been no dramatic change in human
thought or practice. We're regressing. Returning again to what was as
human history repeats itself. Without the constant of light or truth to
guide us, we've again made ourselves the measure of everything, and in
the process lost our way.

Nature itself rebels against our presumption and arrogance. For far
too long we've made choices that served only the immediate and forgot

legacy. I sense a slow and steady collapse. The surrounding forces exerting themselves are greater than our inward constitution can endure. Families are fragmented, nations are divided, government and financial institutions are crumbling. Creation is not well. Its guardians and keepers have left their posts. If our reckless choices have brought destruction, doesn't it stand to reason we can be part of the restoration? There is only one hope of light coming from this darkness. People must choose to live for something more than the immediate.

This world has contracted and shrunk proportionally as the multiple levels of communication technology have expanded. The globe is networked as the cords that once hung so loosely between cultures and nations are intertwined and tightened. There have never been so many voices speaking at once. There is so much noise and yet so little clarity.

While we are advancing on many fronts, much ground has been lost on others. As the world accelerates, its very core has become unstable. There is no safe base. No place of peace and quiet where all activity stops. We are playing worldwide games with no fail-safe. Games without rules or boundaries are fun only for bullies.

Where Is Home Base?

When I was a child, I would run in the dusk of summer nights playing games. There was hide-and-seek, kick the can, and freeze tag, but no matter what the game, there was always a designated base. It might be a lighted porch or garage, but there was always a place of safety. It was where the game no longer continued to exercise its rules over you. If you were hurt, you could run to base and cry, "Safety!" Home base was where you regrouped and asked questions if you were unsure of how to play. It was the place you aired grievances against those who were cheating. Base was where you ran to elude your opponents. It was a center of safety.

Base was also where you went to quit when the night grew too dark or cold and you heard your mother's voice call you in. I remember many nights walking from the solitary light of base to the glowing warmth of my home.

But what of today? Are there only games with no guidelines? Do we run in the dark with no bases? When we are called in, do we find warmth and light in our homes? Is everyone safe in our homes? Is there laughter inside? Or are the mothers alone and sad? Are the fathers harsh and distant? Or is there no one even there?

The human soul is sick and lonely. We've been entertained for so long by the unreal and untrue, nothing truly real moves us. Atrocities no longer break our hearts as long as we are safe. We may get angry, but then it fades. Children are growing up in atmospheres so hardened they have no capacity for remorse or regret.

Individuals exist without purpose and direction because there is nothing greater in their lives than themselves. There is no compass pointing to true North. Truth is relative as we walk in circles, unable to find our center.

It is hard to find something bigger we can count on. We fear there are no powers that cannot be corrupted and no leader who does not lie. Our fathers leave and our mothers are absent. Families are split because marriage commitments mean nothing.

Center gives perspective. It is not a place of inactivity, even though it may be where you least feel activity's pull. Center is the anchor. It controls the activity swirling around it like the eye of a storm. For far too long, men and women have been off center with no safe base.

The Peace at the Center

I grew up with a manual merry-go-round in the park across the street from my home. My friends and I would take our positions around this suspended disk, grab hold of the rails, and begin to run in circles. Our goal was to make it go as fast as possible and yet still be able to jump on without injuring ourselves. As we ran, our focus was the bar before us. We ran until we feared our legs would give way.

Breathlessly waiting for the moment when each of us would make the precarious leap aboard. Someone would shout, "Now!" and we would all attempt the scramble. If someone faltered, it was understood they should let go. We didn't want anyone to be dragged, and if someone was hurt we stopped.

Once on board, we battled to the middle. It was more difficult than staying on the edge, but those who made it found the journey well worth the effort. We sat back-to-back in a tight inner circle as the world around us spun. I don't remember ever feeling nauseous there . . . I felt suspended. Time stood still as the scenery slipped past. Those on the edge of the merry-go-round became bored before we did and normally jumped off before it actually stopped. But in the center, you remained guessing what would be your last view. Would you stop facing the slide, the swings, or your home?

I feel as though we somehow are again on the merry-go-round of my youth. Only this time it is massive, and each orbit does not slow us; we are accelerating. The most frightening element is the fact that we appear to have developed a wobble. Those who have not found center are having a rough time. Many on the outer fringes are losing their balance and toppling off the edge. We are moving far too fast and don't know how to slow down. If Bible prophecy remains true, there will be no slowing of this trend until the old is made new. In this storm of change, God is awakening His women and drawing us into the center. There we find a place of safety where the pull cannot exercise its force on us. There is a life above rules where love is boundless and everyone can find their way to safety. It is a life fully lived here with an eye on what lies beyond. Heaven-driven, we are freed from the tethers of earth. Rules work only when you are playing games. The time for game playing is over. We've lived this earthbound existence for far too long. God is calling us out from among our petty play and inviting us to lift our eyes to something more.

We have been revolving around an axis that is unstable. We are not men; we are women. Men are not women; they are men. Our gender is our strength. It is our core and center, from which we ultimately find our power.

Why Is Gender So Important?

Know and understand this: Our enemy fears the revelation of God's daughters more than he fears women who act like men. Why would he be afraid of women who behave like men, any more than he would fear men who act like women? When men and women are not true to their cores, both genders are out of sync and removed from their positions of strength. Neither guise frightens him, for he has worked long and hard to confound the strengths and magnify the weaknesses of both sexes. The enemy has always been an expert at twisting and perverting truth in order to divert mankind from the path of life. He does not want us walking toward light and truth, and repeatedly coerces us with deceptive half-truths that push us toward the way of death and darkness. Without God's clear directives, we could find ourselves wandering aimlessly on paths of destruction.

> *Our enemy fears the revelation of God's daughters more than he fears women who act like men.*

> *She gives no thought to the way of life; her paths are crooked, but she knows it not.*   (Proverbs 5:6 NIV)

She knows it not . . . I wonder how long we have walked in the wrong direction and knew it not. It is time we gave thought to the right way of life. This way of life includes men and women separate and beautifully unique in their expressions and purposes. We will find ourselves on pathways of deception anytime we accept a lie as truth. We find ourselves wandering the ways of darkness whenever we refuse the counsel of God's timeless wisdom and spurn it as irrelevant to our day or not applicable to our unique situations. It is foolish to think every path brings you to life, because surely if there is a *way of life,* then there is a *way of death*.

*The path of the righteous is like the first gleam of dawn,
shining ever brighter till the full light of day.*

(Proverbs 4:18 NIV)

Righteous paths lead to greater places of illumination. I would argue our current culture confirms that our present course has led us into ways of increasing darkness. This reveals that the path we now tread is bent toward destruction.

A Closer Look at "Male" and "Female"

Before we go further, it is important to define the words *male* and *female*. These definitions will help refine our approach. I know you might be thinking the understanding of these terms is a given, but with all we see happening, I have to wonder.

Webster's defines the term *male* as "a person bearing an X and Y chromosome pair in the cell nuclei."[1] This means gender is a DNA core issue that does not vary, no matter how the physical exterior may be altered. Culture does not have the power to change our core. *Male* is further defined by the adjectives used to describe men and boys. These include *strength, forthrightness, courage,* and *virility.* The term *virile* carries a suggestion of sexual or procreative potency. All references of *male* ultimately lead to the word *man. Webster's* definition of *man* includes both adult males as well as the human species. Specifically, man has *the ability to initiate conception but not to bear children.*

Now we will turn to the definitions of *female, feminine,* and *woman.* Likewise, *female* is first defined as "a person with two X chromosomes in her cell nuclei."[2] The nuclei are defined as "a central part about which other parts or groups are gathered: core."[3] The term *feminine* is defined as "pertaining to a woman or girl: feminine beauty; feminine dress . . . having the qualities traditionally ascribed to women, such as sensitivity or gentleness."[4] *Webster's* also lists delicacy, gracefulness, and patience, as well as sensitivity to moods, as feminine attributes. This leads to the core term *woman*, which is defined as "adult human beings who are biologically female; that is, capable of bearing offspring."[5]

These definitions immediately bring some things to light. The first is the interdependence between the sexes. I have heard this best described as "interdependent but not interchangeable." Just as stated, the man can initiate conception, but there must be a woman to both carry the life and bring it forth. The woman cannot begin life without the man, and the man cannot complete life without the woman. Please do not be deceived; there is no such thing as a sex- or gender-change operation. There is only an operation that changes sexual function and response. This is because no matter how you rearrange the exterior, you can't change the core chromosomes. Feminine behavior is considered a compliment to a woman but a slight to a man. Men who are labeled "effeminate" are considered moved away from their masculine positions of strength.

These definitions raise some questions as well. Are men the only ones who are strong? Can't men be gentle? Of course women can surely be strong, just as men can be gentle. But neither of these are their core attributes. Men are known for their courage and direct manner, just as women are known for their grace and patience. *Grace* is defined as "elegance, beauty, and smoothness of form or movement." It is further defined as "a capacity to accommodate and forgive as well as extend mercy and favor."[6] All these definitions are in keeping with the scriptural references to woman.

A Woman's Strategic Position

Gender alone does not qualify a man to lead, just as gender alone should not disqualify a woman. According to Scripture, if a man is not strong in virtue, he disqualifies himself regardless of his gender, just as women who were historically virtuous rose above perceived gender limitations. The New Testament outlines these leadership virtues:

> *Gender alone does not qualify a man to lead.*

For an elder must be a man whose life cannot be spoken against. He must be faithful to his wife. He must exhibit self-control, live wisely, and have a good reputation. He must enjoy having guests in his home and must be able to teach. He must not be a heavy drinker or be violent. He must be gentle, peace loving, and not one who loves money. He must manage his own family well, with children who respect and obey him.

(1 Timothy 3:2–4 NLT)

Notice the preeminence given to "faithful to his wife." This is first in the long list of qualities accorded a blameless life. Included in this list is being "gentle," an attribute usually ascribed to women. This confirms that there is a marriage of the two strengths, but this can happen without either compromising their core.

Likewise, their wives must be reverent, not slanderers, temperate, faithful in all things. (1 Timothy 3:11 NKJV)

Here women are equally charged to be temperate and faithful. They are encouraged to be an example of virtue.

In this life, everyone has his or her strategic position and place to function. Now let's impose this dynamic on the field of battle. If those charged with guarding the supplies leave their posts unguarded and vulnerable because they want to be part of an offensive assault, the entire army's future strength, security, and provisions are compromised. If the ones skilled in tending the wounded leave their ministrations of healing to protect the store of supplies, who will bring healing and strength to the injured and discouraged? If those who are trained for the front lines run back to attempt to administer healing and prescribe medicine without the proper training in these practices, the wounded will suffer further injury. Not to mention, the entire forward progression of the battle is compromised and costly ground is lost. In many cases, blood must be shed again to recover what was previously purchased in battle. It is imperative that we each fully realize that none of us, no matter how skilled we may be in our unique areas, are capable of functioning independently of others.

Paul compared and contrasted this interdependence with the function of the human body and how the symphony brings strength to each part. The only reason the many can function as one is that we derive our strength from our Head, Jesus the Christ.

> *From him the whole body, joined and held together by every supporting ligament, grows and builds itself up in love, as each part does its work.*   (Ephesians 4:16 NIV)

As *each* part does its work, the whole is built up in love. The verse does not say "as the women do the men's part" or "as the men do the women's," then we will be built up. It very clearly says each part must *do its work* if the whole is to function properly. For too long the men have been fighting the women's battle, and the women have been fighting the men's. For too long the women have been fighting the men, and the men have been fighting the women. In this state of continual internal conflict, there has been far too much wounding and not enough healing and building.

Rigidity Repels Healing

Competition and power positioning have stripped the body of its connective and supportive tissues as each individual part has separated itself from the whole and vied to be highlighted for a post of greatness. God specifically designed the human body with the inability to function successfully if its members are separated. No matter what the childhood song may say to the contrary, there is no connection of bones without the support of ligaments and tendons.

Believe me, after two shoulder injuries, I have learned the importance of supportive connective tissue. I was careless with an injury, and my ligaments just decided to lock my arm down in an immobile state. It didn't matter how hard my muscles and bones tried to lift my arm, it was not going to happen. This lockdown happened as my body tried to protect what was already injured. There was no synchronized movement until I paid attention to what was weak and brought healing to my shoulder's connective tissue. My neglect in strengthening one area cost me a lot of freedom of movement in another. The only way for my movement to be restored was for the adhesions or scar tissue to be stretched. The rigidity had to be addressed in order for there to be healing. When it comes to women functioning in the body, our rigid views must be addressed.

> *He has made us competent as ministers of a new covenant— not of the letter but of the Spirit; for the letter kills, but the Spirit gives life.* (2 Corinthians 3:6 NIV)

First, it is Christ who has made us competent ministers of the new covenant. The new way of life and love has replaced the letter of the fallen perspective. There should no longer be a wrestling match between man and woman, for Christ has made us one. But if this truth is not administered, our movement and function within the body of Christ will remain limited. Returning to the example of my shoulder injury, I fear we have neglected to bring healing to the women. This is crucial because it is often women who function as the connectors or support system in the body. With this statement I am not implying men cannot function in this role, or that women are limited only to this role. I am only reemphasizing that women, by intent, were ultimately created for relationship.

Second, too often we fail to empower women to function in their gifts. Without this crucial ability to properly relate to and support one another, the body will remain disjointed or crippled.

Connection Is Key

Though men and women are equal before God, they are not completely independent of each other. Both genders function best when connected with each other in one way or another. This is not limited to marriages but encompasses all relationships in life. God the Father declared the man alone was not good or complete. If in fact the one (woman) completes the other (man), then it is foolish for the one (man) to spurn the other (woman) as inferior or unnecessary. Both the man and the woman are necessary reflections of God's complete picture. But when the uniqueness of these parts is removed, the image in this picture is blurred and indistinct. For example, if the men function in 90 percent of the roles while the women function in only 10 percent, we have a problem.

John and I love to process things together because we are so different. He has perspective I lack, and I have a vantage he is missing. As we approach interpersonal problems, John will just want to conquer and let the dead lie where they fall! This is not my approach. I will be thinking in terms of how this interaction will affect the future of the relationship. More often than not, the answer is found in a healthy marriage of both perspectives. (Yes, there have been times when I wanted to sever heads, and John stayed my arm as well!) Without separate and distinct honor to each perspective, the image is not whole but appears only in part. I love the way my home church approaches it. They see husbands and their wives as a team and appoint them both as elders regardless of who was actually elected. They do this because they know they will ultimately process decisions as a couple anyway.

In the midst of this struggle for identity and purpose, our homes have lost their atmosphere of love, nurture, instruction, healing, and provision. Some forces in Christendom have attempted to settle the struggle by removing women from any part or role. The answer has never been for the woman to have *no part*, just as it is not for the woman to have *the man's part*; but rather, the woman is to have her own part.

Even now you may find yourself feeling a bit defensive at my words. Please understand, I am not even implying that either men or women are solely at fault in this struggle. I truly believe there has been much wrong done on both sides. The devastation of the lies has worked its destruction on both the males and the females as it has lured us off the path of life.

It's Time to Move On

At times it may appear as though I think women are the only ones needing correction or direction. But I do not have the ear of the men; I am whispering in the ear of the women. Often when I am speaking to one of my children and explaining an adjustment that needs to be made on their part, they are so busy wondering what I will say to their brother that they never even hear my words. God brings direction to His body as a whole, then gives specific correction to the men and women individually. This is a woman-specific message. I don't know about you, but I hear so much better when I know I am being spoken to directly and no one else is listening in.

As a woman I, too, have been misjudged, misrepresented, mistreated, and misunderstood. Even with all this, I beg you to lay aside all the hurt and disappointment and move forward.

I have not always felt this way. I have often thought, *If only I were a man, things would be so much easier.* If I were a man, I would not be judged so harshly. If I were a man, my voice would be heard. If my voice resonated with masculine strength, my children would listen quicker. The truth is, my children actually listen to me a whole lot more when I speak as their mother than when I try to imitate the boisterous voice of their father. When I felt dishonored and overwhelmed by the lack of opportunity for women, I allowed it to propel me deeper into the pursuit of my heavenly Father.

As far as this struggle goes, it is not isolated to the male-female dynamic but seems to be a recurring theme since the announcement of the concept of the many being one body in Christ.

> *And if the ear should say, "Because I am not an eye, I do not belong to the body," it would not for that reason cease to be part of the body. If the whole body were an eye, where would the sense of hearing be? If the whole body were an ear, where would the sense of smell be? But in fact God has arranged the parts in the body, every one of them, just as he wanted them to be.* (1 Corinthians 12:16–18 NIV)

Let us take some liberties with the above example Paul used for the sake of clarification. Following is my paraphrase of the above passage:

> *And if the* woman *should say, "Because I am not a* man, *I do not belong to the body,"* she *would not for that reason cease to be part of the body. If the whole body were* male, *where would the sense of* feminine *be? If the whole body were* female, *where would the* masculine *be? But in fact* God *has arranged the parts in the body, every one of them, just as he wanted them to be.*

Made for the Deep, Not the Shallow

Believe me, there have been many occasions when I have questioned God's sense of wisdom on this one. There have been times when I felt I was much better equipped to play the role of the dominant and outspoken male rather than the more demure and subdued female.

There have even been times when I wanted to distance myself from the whole dynamic of female because of the petty politics and gossip rampant in groupings of females. I feared if I befriended females, I would risk being swallowed up in their world of pink fluff and superficial conversations. Despising all the weaknesses I associated with the female gender, I leaned toward the male dynamic. But then a question arose within me. Perhaps what I rejected as "female fluff" was never originally part of the female DNA. Perhaps I did not like the passive-aggressive behavior for a reason. Maybe I was meant as a woman to despise all the focus on looks and name-dropping because I was originally made not for the shallow, but for the deep. Perhaps I had mistaken the quiet women for the weak. Maybe there were times when more could be heard in a woman's whisper than in a man's shout.

> *Maybe there were times when more could be heard in a woman's whisper than in a man's shout.*

There is an amazing combination found when you marry strength with beauty, authority with wisdom, male with female. It was always God's idea . . . two with one heart. Together, we realize a multiplication of our strengths.

If you were to arrange a contest of physical strength between the largest and most physically powerful woman and the largest and most physically powerful man, who would win? Although I hate to say it, the man, of course, would win. So when it comes to physical strength, why is the playing field not level? The man's strength was never meant to be used *against* woman, but *for* her. Superior strength was given to men to protect and provide for the women in their lives. This strength was never meant to be an instrument of domination or abuse. Weak, confused, powerless men abuse women.

Wherein lies the woman's power if not in her physical strength? We will explore the answer to this question in the remainder of this book.

Heavenly Father,

Reveal my unique strengths, gifts, and value. Restore truth to my inmost parts. I want to lose the wobble. I want the orbit of my life to lend strength to all within the sphere of my influence. I want that safe base, that home where the rules no longer exert themselves upon me. I want to embody all I was fashioned and formed to be and to bring into this earth. I want to be a connecter in the body to bring strength and freedom of movement to every limb. I want to express the heart of a woman. Amen.

CHAPTER FIVE

Who's the Man?

I love to ask my sons this question. Especially after they've experienced a conquest of some type. "Way to go! Who's the man?!"

In response, they flash a quick smile at their loud mom as if to say, "I am so glad you noticed!" It is just a brief interchange that may include a high five, but it always serves to affirm them. I love my sons. Even beyond my ability to express in words. At times it will spill over into neck bites, huge kisses, and rib-crushing hugs. I feel as though I can't get enough of them, and I am always attempting to somehow merge with them. It all started when, as newborns, they looked my way or responded for the first time to the sound of my voice. They each have awakened unique affection and aspects of nurture in my life. One invites me to relax and sit with him awhile. Another prompts me to seek him out. There is one who calls loudly, challenging me to play fearlessly. And yet another shares deep communion of thoughts, feelings, and fears.

I cannot help but see in each of my sons a portion of another man.

Actually, He is the only One I feel could literally and accurately be called "the Man."

When young girls or single women imagine their lives as postponed or empty, I remind them that there is "the Man." He alone is worthy of all our trust, affection, and submission. He is altogether lovely and ever faithful even when we are faithless. Of course I speak of the Man Jesus, who was kind enough to walk this earth as the Son of man. Jesus loved women and allowed them intimate contact in uncomfortable situations. Whether speaking to a woman shunned by others as she drew water from the well or allowing Himself to be anointed in the midst of judgment, He never pulled away.

When Mary sat at His feet, He would not allow the busy Martha to remove her.

He is the only man who will never disappoint you. Even as He was dying, He thought of a woman.

> *"Dear woman, here is your son," and to the disciple, "Here is your mother." From that time on, this disciple took her into his home.*   (John 19:26–27 NIV)

But Jesus' mother was not the only woman He thought of in that moment of pain . . . He was thinking of you. He could not imagine life without you, so He willingly surrendered His earthly life to give you life eternal. I remember the day and the hour when I found this irresistible love. Was it true that He died so I could be His? How could He love one so angry and filthy? What other man had ever shown such love and dedication? Who had ever spoken so tenderly to me? When had I ever been forgiven so completely? He offered me everything in exchange for my broken body and empty, hardened heart. Before Him, my life was a series of shallow gasps, but when His love flooded my being, it was as though I could breathe deeply at last.

God Is Not a Man

He is the only One every woman, single or married, can freely allow to measure her value and worth. He alone is worthy of our lives. God never meant for women to get their life from men. He meant us to get our life from Him. Though Jesus came as the Son of man, He is the Son of God as well. He is more than a man, even though He is overtly masculine in His personality or portrayal. I cannot even begin to tell you the number of women I have spoken with who are afraid of approaching God as a Father. For that matter, they fear anything with a semblance of being male because of what men in their past have done. Let these words bring comfort to you . . . God is not a man.

Take a breath. No, I am not saying He is a woman. He is far more than either a man or a woman, and He is the source of life to all. It's just a fact that people blow it all the time, but not God. What? Are you telling me you've never found yourself disappointed by another? Have you never been cheated? How about lied to? Hurt, betrayed, or used? If you have been alive for any length of time, most likely you have experienced one, if not all, of these painful interactions. No one, no matter how cunning, isolated, or independent, is immune to this reality of imperfect relationships. I know beyond a doubt that I have failed at one time or another in practically every area of life. I have disappointed family and friends. I've been a source of pain to others. Even so, far too often I have looked to man to be the source of things God alone could supply. To move forward as women, it is imperative that we all learn to successfully navigate and steward this truth.

Not long ago, I was traveling to speak at a conference and found myself in the Dallas airport with some time to spare. I was browsing the latest topics in the magazine section, when my attention was arrested by a popular women's magazine that declared "Men and Their Pursuit" as the main feature for the month. Every article addressed one dynamic or another of how females could interact with males. If memory serves, the magazine offered information on the cities with the highest male populations, where to locate them in the cities; how to attract their attention, how to talk to the man once you had it; how to love the man and how to know if the man loved you, etc. As a woman who lives with five males, I am always open to resources. I had picked up the magazine and began to scan its pages, when I heard the Holy Spirit whisper, *But I am not a man.*

I was riveted by the simplicity of this revelation. All our energy is too often spent on a mere reflection of the truest source. For all the independence these women's magazines espouse, they still enthrone the harmonious relationship of a man and a woman as the answer to personal happiness. Yes, there is fulfillment in an intimate relationship with a man, but they are not our answer. Truly, *God is not a man,* and what we ultimately desire will never be completely met or found in one.

Similar, Yet Different

I believe this truth is confirmed by the counsel we find in the book of Numbers:

> *God is not a man . . .*   (23:19 NIV)

This actually declares more than we have the capacity to understand. He is similar yet altogether different from a man or a woman. While both male and female reflect His image, it is a limited one at best. This is comparable to how a mirror can reflect the outward appearance but not the heart . . . the movement of our mouths but not the sounds of our words. At first it may appear as though God is stating the obvious. You may read this verse and think, *Yes, of course I know God is not a man.* But let's pause a moment and review this truth in light of our culture, and we may be surprised to find out just how prevalent this misconception has become.

If we are honest, we will find we inadvertently declare man our "god" on multiple levels. This is expressed in how we spend our money, our time, and our energies. Advertising preys upon our desire to be in a relationship by suggesting if we look and dress like *this* (the desirable woman), we will get *that* (the man of our dreams). We are invited to costume balls where only the perfect and beautiful ultimately win (think Cinderella, perfect car, perfect dress, perfect hair and accessories, completed by amazing shoes). Our trust is misplaced in what draws our affections and drives our desires. We unwittingly buy into this misconception as we pursue "the man" as the solution to every woman's woe. The underlying message, "The perfect man = the perfect life," puts way too much pressure on everyone involved! There is no such thing as a perfect man (or woman); there is only a perfect God.

Married women, how many of you got the man only to find out that no matter how wonderful he is, he cannot fulfill every dimension of your life? With high hopes of perfection and happiness, most women marry the man of their dreams and watch the dream slowly morph into a nightmare! Desperate to keep the dream alive, they attempt to train the man, radically change the man, and if these methods don't work, they just decide to be the man! Believe me, I know this drama firsthand. Shortly after I married my husband, the love of my life, I had a vision for his perfection. It is one I have found to be common among newlywed wives . . . it is the vision of a perfect man.

Inspired, I imagined my life purpose was to *change* John from the man he was into the man I knew he could be, if he would just work with me. With this revelation, everything changed. No longer was I kind and patient; I was focused. There was transformation to be accomplished. For what other possible reason could the gift of such an exacting critical nature have been given me? There were flaws waiting to be addressed. Somehow they had escaped my notice when we dated, but as soon as we were married, these shortcomings became glaringly apparent (as my own flaws receded into obscurity, of course). My life was truly a gift to John's . . . it was obvious—I could be so helpful! Why was I so driven to change and perfect him? I obviously had made him my source of joy and fulfillment.

My Way, or I Won't Play

When we'd first met, I loved John for who he was. But then my affections changed and focused on my expectation of who he could be. If I could change him into this image, I would be safe, loved, and fulfilled. This new perspective was evidenced by comments I would make, such as, "I wouldn't do it that way; I would do it this way." The concept that John should do things *my way* began to flow so naturally and insistently through my being, it dominated my thoughts. What had begun almost gently became more and more persistent as my zeal to change John increased. It was my wifely duty and noble obligation to train John up in the way I felt he should go.

But it just wasn't working! I love how a godly woman named Devi Titus put this into perspective: "Most women serve their children and train their husbands, rather than the other way around." At the time, I didn't have any children, but I was definitely practicing on my husband.

When John resisted my constant and rigorous attempts at training him, I unwittingly thought it best to displace him (at least until he would cooperate). After all, I had repeatedly proved my merit in leadership. How many times had I obviously advised him correctly, and yet he had stubbornly refused to listen? Perhaps things would go more smoothly if I could just "be the man" until he followed my lead. John was not willing to be the woman, so this actually meant we had two leaders going two different directions and divided on just about everything.

Needless to say, this wrestling competition did a lot of damage early in our relationship. It didn't stop until I found out I was looking for John to be things only God could be to me. I was expecting him to be perfect, when clearly none of us are. When he disappointed me, I withdrew my love and respect until he could somehow prove himself worthy again. In those early years, I was afraid of so many things that I tried to control everything.

I bought into the lie that God was a man, and if the man would just try hard enough, he could meet all my needs. But this is not true, for even

> *There are promises made that only God can keep.*

if John had been perfect there are needs in each of us only God can meet. Blaise Pascal said, "There is a god-shaped hole in the life of every man." We were designed to find our ultimate purpose in God alone. There are promises made that only God can keep.

God Cannot Lie

God is not a man, that He should lie. (Numbers 23:19 NKJV)

What is the next obvious takeaway? Men lie. Before you get all angry and wounded over this, remember, women lie too. But God cannot, because He is Truth. People sometimes lie even when they believe they are telling the truth. They may say they will never leave you, and then they do. They may say they will always love you, and then they don't.

Actually, all the lying can become a bit alarming; and it should be a relief to all of us, male and female alike, that God is not like us. God is God, and there is no one like Him. Only He is the faithful and true witness. His perspective is not skewed or obscured by this earthly realm. He cannot be bribed or deceived.

Another way we elevate man to the god-level is when we mistakenly believe people are the source of security and promotion. This could happen when we expect friends to meet all our emotional and supportive needs. Further, the mind-set of the "god-man" has infiltrated the business world, where many mistakenly believe networking and name-dropping are the quickest route to favor, promotion, or provision. Those hungry for the approval of man will become users. There is a lot of "Scratch my back, and I'll scratch yours" going on. Résumés are puffed up, and relationships run superficial courses. Those who service their ambitions are included in their circle, while those who are not useful or necessary are rotated out. This same mind-set has affected the church.

Relationships are not viewed as sacred, but rather as a commodity to be exploited. This type of behavior shows displaced trust in others, rather than trust in God. We want God's favor first and foremost.

It is possible to enjoy favor with God and man, but you must always keep it in that order. First seek God's favor, then allow Him to divinely connect you with others. Too often people pursue the favor of man first, but gaining the favor of man does not necessarily secure favor with God.

Favor with God Versus Favor with Man

In order to keep our perspectives healthy, we must understand that favor with people is all about who we are in public. Everything hinges on the public's perception of us. This is usually forged by appearance and achievement. In this arena, the attractive and successful consistently win. When their popularity wavers, they will suffer loss if they tie their worth to people's opinions. God does not waver in His love toward us, no matter what the public's opinion of us may be.

Favor with God is realized in secret. It focuses on who we are in private when no one is around to applaud or cheer. Who we are "off the record" is a much more accurate representation of who we truly are. Almost universally, poor decisions we make in private destroy our favor in public. Are the choices to be involved

> *Favor with God is realized in secret.*

in sinful activities—such as gossip, pornography, adultery, or embezzlement—public or private decisions? Most of these begin in the privacy of our thought-lives. Choices to steal, cheat, or betray are made under the cloak of secrecy.

In private, we also have the ability to cultivate a thought-life that is purified through a right relationship with God. Alone with Him, our motives are weighed and revealed. In His presence, all disappointments and expectations are laid to rest. There I am embraced for who I am, not for what I do. This is the real me, who I am when no one is watching. This is whom God enjoys spending time with the most. In His presence, I find a more accurate reflection because my worth comes from Him alone. Who I am alone with Him is much more important to Him than anything I might accomplish for Him in public.

It's Always Better to Trust God

Sometimes I run into the safety of His presence because I am afraid and have lost perspective. There I am reminded:

> *Fear of man will prove to be a snare, but whoever trusts in the* LORD *is kept safe.*   (Proverbs 29:25 NIV)

And,

> *In God I trust; I will not be afraid. What can man do to me?*
>   (Psalm 56:11 NIV)

The psalmist raises a good question. People will come against you, but what can they actually do if you trust in God? We trust what we believe. If we believe God when He tells us He holds our lives in His hands, then we will find ourselves unafraid of the threats of men.

There have been a number of times when I have been located by what frightened me. Words of gossip and slander swirled around me, and I desperately tried to snatch them back or explain my side of the story. Like most everyone, I hate being misunderstood and misrepresented, but there comes a time when I just have to let it go and trust in God's goodness. We will be misunderstood, misjudged, misrepresented, and mistaken by friends and enemies alike, but never by God.

> *It is better to trust in the* LORD *than to put confidence in man.*
>   (Psalm 118:8 NKJV)

This is not an admonishment to distrust people, but rather a directive of where to place your trust. It is better to totally surrender to God's mercy and fairness than to even think of relying on people who, throughout history, have proved to be consistently unreliable. The only way to trust God more is to know Him better. This can happen as you reflect on His attributes. He is unchanging and righteous. God is the Beginning and the End, our shield and defense. God is Truth. His honor is above question, and His power is limitless. He is altogether different from us.

Love at a Standstill

I want to preface this next story with the fact that I love and respect my husband. This does not mean we always see things eye-to-eye. In more than twenty-three years of marriage, we have definitely butted heads a few times. The consequences were more damaging at some times than others. I share from our life in the hope you may learn from my failings and avoid serious consequences in your own life or marriage.

John and I are both passionate people. This definitely has its upside, but it can just as quickly spiral downward. Passionate people tend to *feel* everything on a large scale. When we find ourselves confronted with heated topics, naturally we both express strong opinions. Out of respect for each other, we've always had the policy of discussing difficult issues first in private before making our voices known in public. In keeping with this in the case of our ministry board meetings, John and I discuss the agenda first at home to avoid any unpleasant surprises.

We've found this practice saves us both undue embarrassment and hurt feelings. Well, a number of years ago something went very wrong in a board meeting. Due to a number of factors, a project was introduced for a vote that I knew nothing about. I immediately felt violated and betrayed, especially when I realized I was the only board member who had not previously been advised on the matter. In addition to this, I was the only female, so it seemed I had been left out of the boys' club. When the time came to vote, every other board member voted yes, but I gave a resounding "No!" Actually, I think I even raised my hand to emphasize my opposition.

I wasn't going to take this violation lying down! The sad thing was, our board had always voted unanimously until that day, but at the time I just didn't care. I disagreed. If I wasn't free to vote no, then I wasn't free to vote yes. The measure passed even without my vote, but I imagined I had done something honorable and, of course, very patriotic.

As you can imagine, John had a very different outlook on my behavior. After the board meeting, a heated discourse began that we were not able to successfully finish before John left for two back-to-back international trips. The distance and time did nothing to help resolve the conflict. Both of us only dug our heels in deeper and defended our decisions vehemently. I felt victimized, and John felt resisted and dishonored. Because we were in such an intense standoff, we both kept gathering ammunition to support our individual positions. We argued and spoke with everyone we thought might be of help, but there was no sign of any resolution in sight.

Desperate, I began to cry out to the Lord, "God, we are at a standstill. John is not being nice at all! Father, I know You must be upset by his behavior; after all, he is dealing treacherously with the wife of his youth!" On and on I went; almost daily I made my case before the Father. But when I was finally quiet, I heard Him speak: *Lisa, tell Me I'm enough for you.*

At first I was a bit frightened. If I said God was enough, did that mean John wasn't going to change? I echoed back the words: "Father, You're enough for me."

Then I found myself repeating the question. "But what about John?"

Again I heard, *Tell Me I am enough for you.*

"You're enough for me."

At first my response was just words. Words I knew I should say. Not the words I felt like saying. They just became the only words I knew to say that would not get me into trouble. If God was enough for me, I did not need to gather everyone else's opinions. If God was enough for me, I didn't have to worry about all the ways I saw John as not enough. If God was enough, then disappointment in friendships no longer mattered or determined my ability to forgive. I began to murmur these words in the dark of my closet, in the silence of my car, and whispered them when I went to bed at night. Then something happened. God was no longer enough—He became *more than* enough for me. This revelation began to spill out in my praise and soon overtook my need to be right.

Take the Truth; Leave the Lie

As God was exalted, the entire posture of my life changed, and love overtook our marriage. The truth is, no husband can meet all his wife's needs, nor be the healing agent of all her wounds. Sure, your husband can love and encourage you. Friends can inspire you and bring you joy by just being with them. But all human relationships are limited reflections of His perfect love. God is our true source of joy, contentment, and worth. He alone can define who we are. No one else should have that power. Only in Christ can we find all we are meant to be.

It is an odd but common human practice to return to a source of pain for healing. Sadly, this means we often set ourselves up to be hurt again. For example, a young girl who cannot seem to please her father will often grow up seeking the company of men who are hard to please. She hopes that through the process of winning their approval, she will ultimately realize healing from her father's rejection. Victims of sexual abuse frequently become sexual abusers or promiscuous in an attempt to recover the power that was stolen from them when they were young.

There is no true healing to be found in these places. But far too often, frail humans exchange the truth for the lie, the substance for the shadow, life for death.

> *They exchanged the truth of God for a lie, and worshiped and*
> *served created things rather than the Creator—who is forever*
> *praised. Amen.*   (Romans 1:25 NIV)

If we have in any way exchanged the truth for a lie, then we can in fact decide to exchange our lies for His truth. It all begins with telling God the Father He is Truth; He is our source of worth and more than enough for us. Let's pray together now.

Heavenly Father,

Forgive me for believing the lie that I could find true life and love out-side You. You are the way, the truth, and the life. Holy Spirit, reveal every area where I have exchanged truth for a lie. I want You above all else. Jesus, You are more than enough for me. You are truly not a man that You should lie. You have promised and will keep Your word. I want Your favor more than I want popularity with others. Restore a healthy balance to my life as I renew my mind with who I am in You. Amen.

CHAPTER SIX

When Do Women Strike?

I have noticed a recurring theme or pattern throughout the Bible. The principles of timing, method, and approach worked when employed by a wide range of heroines, from the nameless to the royal. These women repeatedly portrayed *how, why,* and *when* we are to fight.

Let's first tackle the issue of *when.* Women strike when the enemy draws near. Whenever Satan trespasses the boundaries of love and life and comes within range, it is not us, but he, who should tremble. For when we find ourselves ensnared in unavoidable conflict, God will strengthen us to fight with whatever is in our hands.

King Abimelech discovered this truth the hard way. After he successfully surrounded a city, he set fire to all who sought refuge within its tower. Emboldened by his success, he approached yet another city to destroy it in a similar manner. Once again the terrified people ran for refuge within their tower, and Abimelech drew near to kindle the fire, never doubting his victory. The only problem was, on this occasion there was a woman who understood it was time for him to be stopped with whatever she had in hand.

> *Abimelech went to the tower and stormed it. But as he approached the entrance to the tower to set it on fire, a woman dropped an upper millstone on his head and cracked his skull. Hurriedly he called to his armor-bearer, "Draw your sword and kill me, so that they can't say, 'A woman killed him.'" So his servant ran him through, and he died. When the Israelites saw that Abimelech was dead, they went home.*
>
> (Judges 9:52–55 NIV)

What this woman began, a man finished. If the millstone had not been dropped, this bloodthirsty, ruthless king would not have been run through by his armor-bearer's sword. I find it amazing that an entire army, who were ready to burn alive their fellow countrymen, simply went home when they realized their king was dead. He was the force behind their fight, but when they saw him dropped by a woman, they backed off their whole campaign. Could it be that when this man fell before a woman, they knew God was fighting for His people?

Of course we all know women can strike, wound, and kill just like a man, but is it our highest purpose? I believe women were never designed to seek out physical conflict on literal battlefields with men, but if they find themselves thus engaged, they become formidable adversaries. As I will explain in the pages of this chapter, there are plenty of other fields for us to fight on. Involving women in bloodshed and the crossing of swords is always a last resort. Our reasons behind confrontation need to be motivated by what preserves life, honor, truth, and virtue. Both genders should choose battles wisely. If we find conflict in our way that has come to destroy what we guard, then we have no choice but to fight with whatever means we find available. When evil presents itself and blocks our paths, there is no other recourse for the daughters of Eve. We were formed to do all within our power to prevent death and loss, as well as to promote the dignity and preservation of life and virtue. In these pursuits, we must never foolishly draw back in fear.

Women Fight Differently

I remember as a young girl first glimpsing the powerful truth that *women fight differently* as I read C. S. Lewis's classic *The Lion, The Witch and the Wardrobe.* Father Christmas was giving gifts to the sons of Adam and the daughters of Eve in preparation for a long-awaited battle between the powers of good and evil. This confrontation came on the heels of a dreadful season of cold and barrenness. Now spring was exerting itself upon the winter season, and the awaited release was at hand. But first the good of the long-withheld Christmas was brought forth. Each gift was chosen according to the recipient's capacity and compassion. Peter was presented with a magnificent sword and an emblazoned shield. Then the daughters of Eve, Susan and Lucy, were given their gifts each in turn.

> *"Susan, Eve's daughter," said Father Christmas. "These are for you," and he handed a bow and a quiver full of arrows and a little ivory horn. "You must use the bow only in great need," he said, "for I do not mean you to fight in the battle. It does not easily miss. And when you put this horn to your lips and blow it, then, wherever you are, I think help of some kind will come to you."[1]*

There is some interesting symbolism in this passage. First, she is given the gift of a bow and a full quiver of arrows. It is interesting to note the Bible compares our children to arrows in hand.

> *Like arrows in the hands of a warrior are sons born in one's youth.* (Psalm 127:4 NIV)

Women intimately partner with God as they bear and raise children. They are our seed and His heritage and reward. They are the ones we launch into the future. They live far beyond us with eyes that see up close what we see only far off. Their ears will hear out loud things that were only sounded as a whisper in our lifetimes. They are to be carefully aimed and propelled, for they will not easily miss their marks. We are promised that, by raising them in the way they should go, they will be more inclined to hit the target of their destiny in God when they are grown.

For this reason, our children should never be held back by our fears. Necessary battles await them. They have the power to make peace or continue unresolved conflict. They alone hold fast and carry into the future what we have already won on their behalf. In battles of old, arrows were used as a form of advance attack. This means they were often released even before the two armies were in position to be engaged. Likewise, our children are sent to fight in a future we may never see.

Make Use of Available Help

In this manner of advance warning, the second gift to Susan, daughter of Eve, was rather like the first. It was a beautiful horn that when trumpeted brought certain help. It was promised to bring aid, no matter where Susan found herself. What would you do with a gift so lovely and certain? Most of us would readily answer, "Use it!"

But do you know you possess a more sure promise from the Father? No, it is not a tangible ivory horn or a whistle to hang around your neck. Your gift is both invisible and intangible, and in this there is great benefit. It can never be damaged, stolen, or misplaced. Our surety of this is found in His living Word that endures forever. The One who listens for our call is the Holy One, who neither sleeps nor slumbers. It is He who promises to answer our cries for help. In fact, He sets the answers to our problems in motion even before we call for help.

Before they call I will answer; while they are still speaking I will hear. (Isaiah 65:24 NIV)

Before we lend breath to our prayers, He has prepared both wise counsel and a way of escape from harm. If Susan, after being entrusted with such a great and powerful gift, failed to use it, would we not think her foolish? If she despised the horn because it was not a sword, everyone would suffer for her mistaken perceptions. But we unwittingly do this all the time. We forget the gifts God has promised us as His daughters, and we remain silent when our voices should be raised. We foolishly compare our gifts with the gifts of others, and deem ours weak or inferior by comparison. At other times, we look at the futility of our situations and imagine God's ability is not sufficient to tackle the messes we've made. Know this: there is a battle, the damage is extensive, and it is no longer about us.

> *Know this: there is a battle, the damage is extensive, and it is no longer about us.*

Just as Susan was promised help of some kind, our answers more often than not will come in unexpected ways. In my own life, I have found God's intervention to be the exact gift of assistance *I needed* at the time, but not always what *I wanted*. Of course, I realize this only by way of hindsight. Many times I have imagined or contrived an entirely different method, scenario, and timing for the anticipated help. Perhaps I wanted someone to apologize to me, but instead God prompted me to humble myself and apologize to them. At other times I felt a desperate need to defend myself, and God let me know I was to be still and know He is God. He would be my defense, but that meant I would have to keep my hands off if I wanted His involvement.

All We Have to Do Is Ask

*Call to Me, and I will answer you, and show you great and mighty
things, which you do not know.* (Jeremiah 33:3 NKJV)

Being human, I have always called out to God from my limited realm of
what I know. In my desperation, I just wanted immediate help. But God
has a bigger purpose in mind, and He answers us from His limitless domain of the unknown and yet to be seen. In His wisdom, He promises to
reveal great and mighty things to all who simply trust enough to call out
to Him. It is in this place of trust we discover that His riches are to be
found in the midst of our distress. All we need to do is ask Him to get
involved.

Susan's horn interpreted her cry for help by composing a signal she
could not create with human breath alone. Likewise, when we lend our
breath in prayer, the Holy Spirit intercedes on our behalf and presents a
heavenly sound before our Father. Too often, we miss all this adventure
and excitement because we are afraid to trust Him, so we attempt an alternative rescue of our own. I am all for self-help, but it is important to
understand that if you are the only one involved in the equation, the solution doesn't get any bigger than you. God is always the bigger, better
answer.

There has never been a more exciting time to be alive. Through the resources of communication, the truth of the gospel has never been so ac-
cessible. The songs of worship and praise have never been more relevant
and powerful. The light is increasing as the darkness spreads. Yet at the
same time, it feels as though the lies of the enemy have never loomed so
large nor held so vast an array under their sway. We are poised for a battle
of overwhelming proportions! Though the odds may be against us, our
God is for us! We need to trust that He has already made a way, and in
prayer we should confidently sound the horn when we see danger looming.

Let's return to the presentation of gifts and see what is entrusted to
the second daughter of Eve, Lucy.

The Way God Uses Women's Valor

*He gave her a little bottle of what looked like glass (but peo-
ple said afterwards that it was made of diamond) and a small
dagger. "In this bottle," he said, "there is a cordial made of
the juice of one of the fire-flowers that grow in the mountains
of the sun. If you or any of your friends are hurt, a few drops
of this will restore you. And the dagger is to defend yourself
at great need. For you also are not to be in the battle."*

*"Why, Sir," said Lucy. "I think—I don't know—but I think
I could be brave enough."*

*"That is not the point," he said. "But battles are ugly when
women fight."*[2]

In Lucy's reaction I saw so much of my own. I expected Susan to be
content with her gifts and happy to be uninvolved in battle, but not Lucy.
I remember being profoundly disappointed by the answer she received.
This was not because it was wrong; I just wasn't sure it was enough. I remember thinking, *Why not the gift of a sword and shield?* I knew Lucy
would never fail to prove herself brave and true. How could the noble
sword or another weapon of assault and power be withheld? All she
wanted was a chance to prove her love for Aslan. Why was she not allowed the chance?

As I have traveled farther down this path of life, this question has remained. So many women desperately long to prove their love. They are
willing to do whatever is necessary to see their Lord honored in every
facet of life. If our valor is not the issue, what is the point? I have found
myself echoing Lucy's self-doubt: "Jesus, I don't know, but I think I
could be brave enough. Jesus, please let me help in a significant way. I
won't be tacky and ugly in battle, just tell me it isn't because I would fail
You if I were put to the test and thrown into the mix."

For some reason, I always saw the differences in gender roles as some
undeniable flaw on my part. I imagined an infraction or insurmountable

breach had occurred simply because I was female. Too frequently, I sat ashamed of my feminine gender as I heard it repeatedly suggested that women were bent toward wrong and therefore must be relegated to positions where they would do the least harm. Too often I had heard women portrayed as weak and rebellious and therefore allowed only delegated positions of limited and very controlled authority.

But what if the reason for our differences was never one of fault? What if it was because God never meant women to be instruments of death and destruction? Then this role variance would not be due to some inherent weakness or failure on the part of women, but due to a difference in purpose. Problems arise when women are not empowered to freely function in their giftings and strengths.

Warriors for Life

We have drawn such negative conclusions only because we have looked through eyes shadowed by the Fall. It is apparent that even now we wrestle with the roles of men as our goal or source of strength. If we are like them, we are strong; if we are different, we are weak. The very genesis of life established the idea that the contribution of woman, no matter in what form, was never wrong; it was right. What has become wrong is our attempt to garner strength in the form and function of men and neglect our strength as women. The other wrong has come through men devaluing the women's role outside their role.

Rather than presenting us as a problem to be controlled, God created women as an answer to be embraced. I think God always intended us for a higher purpose than a warrior of bloodshed . . . He formed us as warriors for life. Tell me, is it nobler to stretch forth your hand to strike and wound, or to administer healing? What is more valuable, taking life or

> *Rather than presenting us as a problem to be controlled, God created women as an answer to be embraced.*

elevating it? Is there more power to be found in laying siege to a city or in feeding an enemy? There are many ways to wage battles without bloodshed, as the book of Proverbs tells us:

> *A gentle tongue can break a bone.*   (25:15 NIV)

And to divert injury,

> *A gentle answer turns away wrath.*   (15:1 NIV)

The victory does not always fall to the physically strongest. Enemies often crumble before the influence of wisdom. Women, we have fought for too long as men, and whether we truly realize it or not, all have suffered great loss through our struggles. Our children have suffered as they have witnessed this wrestling of the sexes. It is time for us to stop fighting the men. It is time for the women to stop fighting one another. We must recapture our stature of wisdom and again win.

There have definitely been times when I did not model the gentle tongue in conversations. We have all seen women behaving badly. The truth is, we all know women can hurt and even kill others. Our mistake comes in thinking of this as a position of power.

It is said that even though Joan of Arc rode into battle and was heralded a warrior, she never wielded a sword or struck an enemy. Why call her a warrior? What purpose did she serve? She understood her presence on the battlefield was not for bloodshed, but for life. She held high the banner of freedom and lifted the hopes of France heavenward.

In life's battles, if all are engaged in combat, who upholds the standard? Who uplifts the honor and purpose behind the struggle? When all are engaged in bloodshed, we soon forget why we fight. When the war is over, who comforts the weary and gives them a place to lay their heads, if not the women? Who chases away the images of horror and gives back dreams of life and hope? I believe these are powerful roles God has entrusted His daughters to fulfill.

Is My Contribution Enough?

Lucy is given a diamond vessel filled with a cordial of rare liquid that promises to bring healing. It is a priceless gift, yet she is disappointed. Perhaps she imagined it a trinket. Maybe the beauty of the item caused her to doubt it had any real power or purpose. Imagine the great need for such a treasure as this. She is given a chance to heal herself and bring healing to others, and yet she wonders if her contribution is enough. I think at this moment we are posed a similar question. Will our gift be powerful enough? Will our portion be potent enough? Can we believe God crafted women for good and placed them in the kingdom for such a time as this?

Will we continue to doubt the value of our gifts because we view them through the eyes of a gender-confused culture? As daughters of Eve, we have the power to change our world with our gifts of love and life.

The liquid in Lucy's cordial is extracted from a flower that grows on the slopes of the mountains of the sun. This description brought immediately to my mind the poetic picture of healing found in the book of Malachi:

> *The Sun of Righteousness shall arise with healing in His wings.* (4:2 NKJV)

Within her grasp is a liquid born of light and fire squeezed from living beauty. I have to wonder, was this liquid deep and crimson? It is so potent only a drop is necessary to effect great healing.

In addition to this, Lucy is also given a dagger. I am certain she felt the blade too short in its reach. She would willingly plunge headlong into battle and die if needed, and all she is offered is a gift of self-protection. I imagine she wanted something grander and more sweeping in its arc than this puny length of steel small enough to fit in the palm of her hand. It is light and easily concealed, but she doesn't want it hidden.

She wants everyone to know she fights for her king. But this gift again illustrates our proposition: *When the enemy draws near, the women strike.* I believe it is only when he has come too close that he realizes we are armed with unexpected resources.

The Unexpected Weapon

I have heard women described as "God's secret weapon." I am not sure if we are so much a secret as we are the unsuspected. The lie has spun its web so well, and we have danced on the end of its string for so long, there is no reason to imagine anything will change after so many years of confusion. But even now the enemy of every man, woman, and child tightens the cords, confident his scheme will win. But what will happen when those who have been lied to awaken to the truth that they have been wrestling an ally and listening to an enemy? Remember, in our battle,

We wrestle not against flesh and blood. (Ephesians 6:12 KJV)

The bride will awaken to this truth. The church will arise and cast off their folly. The alarm will be sounded, the women and children will be sent forth equipped, and the cordial of God will bring healing to all His people. Then the enemy will feel both the dagger and the sword, for he has drawn far too near. Each part of the body will be valued for its unique contribution, and each joint will lend its strength. It was only later, in the aftermath of battle, that Lucy fully realized the value of her gift. Like this daughter, we are destined to realize our value when the need for our gift is the greatest:

"Quick, Lucy," said Aslan.

And then, almost for the first time, Lucy remembered the precious cordial that had been given her for a Christmas present. Her hands trembled so much that she could hardly undo

the stopper, but she managed it in the end and poured a few
drops into her brother's mouth.

   "There are other people wounded," said Aslan while she
was still looking eagerly into Edmund's pale face and won-
dering if the cordial would have any result.

   "Yes, I know," said Lucy crossly. "Wait a minute."

   "Daughter of Eve," said Aslan in a graver voice, "others
also are at the point of death. Must more die for Edmond?"[3]

When we doubt the value or power of our gift, like Lucy, we will forget what we have. We will fail to freely serve others as we cling to our
own individual needs and hope it works just for us. When we doubt both
our value as women and the treasure entrusted us, we will not lift our
eyes to others.

Looking Beyond Our Families

Lucy did not come to her senses until she was reminded who she was.
On the battlefield littered with wounded, she was more than Edmund's sister. She was a daughter of Eve and a noble queen who served her people
with her gift. We will never truly recover our power or purpose if our vision is limited. The healing in our hands is first portioned to our families,
then extended beyond us to quicken the lives of others. Don't imagine I am
suggesting we should not faithfully steward our families or marriages. I am
only reminding you they cannot be all we see. Healthy families and individuals reach out. We can become so entangled with our own family dynamics that our world shrinks and contracts in on itself. The virtuous
woman of Proverbs 31 had a healthy understanding of this:

   [She] provides food for her household, . . . she extends her
   hand to the poor, yes, she reaches out her hands to the needy.
   She is not afraid of snow for her household, for all her house-
   hold is clothed with scarlet.   (vv. 15, 20–21 NKJV)

She reaches out, unafraid that by extending her hand her household will suffer loss. Warmth will remain in her house. She is confident in God's provision. When there are wounded, she tends them. She is the connection God uses for the outpouring of His healing cordial. Warmth, healing, and hope are powerful opponents of despair and destruction.

A Time to Fire, a Time for Strategy

I want to talk again about this dynamic of arrows. We fight one way when the enemy is far off and quite differently when he is up close and personal. Women are very intuitive, and we often will sense danger when it is but an approaching shadow in the distance. This is when we have a choice; we can react in panic, or we can act wisely. If we are wise, we will sound the horn and begin shooting arrows of prayer heavenward and let them fall upon our foe while he is yet far off.

Unfortunately, this is not usually our first reaction. Instead of shooting, we talk the problem over with others and allow it to expand and multiply in our minds. Then we lose perspective and drop what we have in our hands. This allows fear to draw us into close contact before we have done our part. In ancient battles, the archers were always called in before the armies met. They were on the scenes long before the battle mired down to hand-to-hand combat. Why? Because what works long range does not necessarily work when the armies are engaged. If arrows were raining down from the sky, there would be far too much friendly fire. So in battle, there is a time to fire the shotgun scatter-shot and a time to be precise and exhibit more strategy.

We see the dynamics of how to fight in the life of Queen Esther, whose story is found in the book of Esther in the Bible. Esther was a weapon of divine precision strategically hidden away in a palace. The following is a recap.

The enemy of God's people was arrogant, and his desire for vengeance had grown insatiable. One Jew would not bow, and Haman's wounded pride would not be satisfied until all Jews were annihilated. This caused him to trespass Esther's territory and overplay his hand. He drew near the king and designed a decree that threatened the lives of her people. Though a queen, Esther realized something most have forgotten: None of us are isolated. If we imagine ourselves untouchable or think our fortresses impenetrable, we will soon see them fall. What we tolerate for others will soon overtake us all. Strength is given for the protection of the weak. When she learned of the pending confrontation, Esther sounded the alarm and released her arrows. She called out to God in fasting and prayer before even meeting the enemy face-to-face.

> *Do not eat or drink for three days, night or day. My maids*
> *and I will do the same. And then, though it is against the law,*
> *I will go in to see the king. If I must die, I am willing to die.*
>   (Esther 4:16 NLT)

Esther has become a key figure and role model for women young and old today. Her story has been retold in books and movies. Could it be God is once again secretly hiding His own in places of influence and power? Is He strategically positioning royal daughters who are skilled in obedience and who understand the fear of the Lord? Are there yet some who will not flinch at the enemy's threats or tremble in the face of death?

Your Status with the King

Just like Esther, you have private influence with your king. This is never something to be taken lightly; it is an entrusted gift. Favor and influence are never our own; they are merely lent to us in this life. If we use these tools wisely, they will not only secure our future but also the futures of those around us.

Esther realized that both her beauty and royal position were for a purpose greater than self-affirmation. In a moment's time, all the pieces came together and she knew the enemy was within the gate. The king had heard Haman's proposal as a chance to strengthen his kingdom, but she knew it for what it really was—a plot to destroy her people. Even now the enemy pretends to say one thing when he is actually threatening quite another.

> *If you keep quiet at a time like this, deliverance for the Jews will arise from some other place, but you and your relatives will die. What's more, who can say but that you have been elevated to the palace for just such a time as this?*
>
> (Esther 4:14 NLT)

We are truly positioned for *such a time as this.* Like Esther, we can no longer remain silent when we see threats and injustice. Esther's gift of wisdom and her banquet of honor elevated a bad decision on the king's part to a good situation for God's people. Instead of experiencing destruction, they turned the tables and destroyed those who sought their lives. Divine retribution had its way, and the mighty and arrogant were cast down, while the meek and wise were exalted. God used a woman to avert the genocide of His people. Her subtle role was ultimately more powerful than the reach of the king. He could not repeal his decree, but Esther found a way to redeem it.

So what of now? Has the enemy drawn near, and you do not strike because you are afraid you do not have what it will take?

Are you fighting for what really matters?

Do you doubt God could anoint a millstone to kill a king?

Have you forgotten you have the promise of help, no matter what the mess or where you find yourself?

Like Lucy, have you wrestled with questions of why you have not been included in the same manner as the men?

Do you even now doubt the value of what you carry in your hand?

Don't! Daughter, you are both strategic and valuable. You are the other side of battle. You are the insight to recognize the enemy's approach. You are the intuition to hear what is really being said in his threats. You are the agent of healing. You are the unsuspected one he will learn to fear. You are the missing piece we all need.

Let's pray,

———————

Heavenly Father,

I come to You in the name of Jesus and by the power of Your Holy Spirit. Please reveal the importance of my position. When I look at myself, I don't see it. But when I lift my eyes and look at the desperate need and devastation surrounding me, I long to have my part. I want to prove my love in every way possible. I will not despise the cordial of healing. I will intercede for life in the face of death. I want to walk in wisdom, insight, intuition, and understanding. I want to enter into the adventure of partnering with You to redeem the attack of the enemy.

I will put my arrows to the string. I will equip my children and send my prayers heavenward. I am Your answer to so many problems; open my eyes to see it clearly. Amen.

———————

CHAPTER SEVEN

Fighting with Wisdom

Shortly after I became a Christian, I experienced this glaring revelation: I was an idiot! Everything I had thought and the reasons for my thoughts were based on human suppositions or even lies. The motivations behind the majority of my decisions and actions were based on faulty information.

Even today, it doesn't take a rocket scientist to realize there is an appalling famine of wisdom in the land. It is quite possible there has never been a generation so filled with educated fools. There are mental geniuses lacking the very basic tenets of common sense or courtesy. Never before has knowledge been so easy to access and research and information more readily available, yet with all our collecting and ingathering there remains a famine of common sense and reason.

We absorb ceaseless information on multiple levels, yet far too often we lack any tangible transformation. Families are broken, marriages are fractured, our judicial system is at times foolish, our leaders often are corrupt, and our teachers are hindered from educating. Evil is called good, and good is called evil. Lies are broadcast as truth, leaders fall, children are afraid, and women are violated. Ministers have lost faith and, far too often, their integrity. Actors, those who merely pretend, are our heroes and role models. At best, our culture is sick and wounded. The family is not healthy, and our global environment teeters in the balance.

As if we did not have enough evidence that our current decisions are wrong, we continue to research and gather more data. We are searching for answers we have already been given.

> *Your many medicines will bring you no healing. The nations*
> *have heard of your shame. The earth is filled with your cries*
> *of despair. Your mightiest warriors will stumble across each*
> *other and fall together.*   (Jeremiah 46:11–12 NLT)

There is something so hopelessly tragic in these words of Jeremiah's. These ancient words could almost describe our time . . . abundant medicines yet no healing, and the meeting of the mighty in battle with no apparent victor. Do we wander in shame because we've lost our way, or did we willfully choose foolishness? When we deliberately leave paths of light to explore the recesses of darkness, often we are too smart to find our way back home.

Recapturing Wisdom

As I've gotten older, I've realized wisdom is not really a function of education. There are brilliant people who are unable to live well and function in what they know. These people have knowledge but not wisdom. Wisdom has the power to transform those who apprehend it. Wisdom could be defined as the intimate embrace of truth, when truth merges with our being and begins to drive and direct our actions.

> *Wisdom could be defined as the intimate embrace of truth.*

There are repeated biblical references to wise women, and wisdom is personified as a woman in the book of Proverbs:

> *Wisdom calls aloud in the street, she raises her voice in the public squares.*   (1:20 NIV)

And,

> *Say to wisdom, "You are my sister."*   (7:4 NIV)

Unfortunately, there is another woman fighting for our attention as well. The world calls her many things—seductive, cunning, controlling—but the Bible calls her wayward. She is the image of this world, and she wants you to conform to her counsel. You find her insights on most of the magazine covers as she promises you power if you embrace her ways, but she lies.

As daughters, how can we recover our name of wisdom? Actually, the apprehension of wisdom may be simpler than you first suspect. It is available to all. I believe there is but one major difference between wise women and foolish women. Do you want to know what it is?

> *Knowing when to let go . . . and when to hold on.*

That's it. Wisdom is always found in this dynamic of exchange. It is almost the equivalent to breathing in the Spirit. Wise women know what to hold fast to and what to release, while foolish women hold on fast to what will kill them and release what would bring them life. Wise women hold on to the promises of God and let go of the things that poison or frustrate life. They let go of bitterness, unforgiveness, anger, pain, fear, jealousy, hatred, turmoil, and the past.

Foolish women just don't get this. They hold on to these things, trying to make someone pay the debts they feel owed. While they cling to the past, they release the very things they should hold: God's promises,

His faithfulness, His character, His love, His forgiving power, and His plans for their futures.

Wise women lay hold of God's promises and let go of life's disappointments. Foolish women hold on to the disappointments as they fight to prove themselves right. Wise women understand you will never win with bitterness and offense as companions. The wise understand you can prove yourself right and ultimately be wrong. After all, do you want to fight, or do you want to win? The wise know how to win without a battle.

I recently found myself in the midst of relational conflict where I repeatedly experienced heartache and frustration. Watching me struggle, John tried to help me regain perspective. "Lisa, what is it that keeps pulling you back into this?"

At first, I honestly did not know. I had forgiven, released, blessed, reasoned, confronted, prayed, and fasted. I had given gifts . . . yet there was one thing I could not come to terms with. I hated that I could not make it right. I had no control over the outcome. No matter what approach I took, the result remained the same.

> As far as it depends on you, live at peace with everyone.
>
> (Romans 12:18 NIV)

You go as far as your power allows, and if nothing changes, you have no choice but to let it go. You bless and move on. You exchange frustration for release. You release what is in your hand so He can release what is in His.

Biblical Women Who Made the Exchange

The Bible includes the stories of a number of women whose lives exemplified this dynamic of exchange. By the power of wisdom, they preserved life, averted destruction, and assured legacy.

Eve

The first on our list is our friend Eve. After overwhelming failure, she let go of death and disappointment and embraced the promise of life beyond her choices. She chose to look forward to what she would never fully see and named her third son Seth, or "Seed," thus reaffirming God's promise. She exchanged death for the hope of redemption.

Sarah

Next I want to highlight Sarah. She chose to leave behind her comfort and travel toward the unknown with her husband, Abraham. Together they looked for something more. For years she suffered the disappointment of barrenness. She'd hoped to give her husband a legacy through a son. She really complicated things by giving Abraham her handmaiden, Hagar, to sleep with, and Ishmael was the result. How many women would go this far to see God's promises fulfilled? I sure would not give another woman my place in bed! Of course this was never what God had in mind for Sarah and Abraham anyway. It was through their son together, Isaac, that God's promise to them both was fulfilled. *Isaac* means "laughter." Sarah had laughed at God's promise of a child with Abraham. But it was not long before she exchanged the laughter of disbelief for the laughter of joy.

We all cheer Abraham as the Father of Faith for receiving the promise, but it was Sarah who carried this baby and delivered it full term. Mother Sarah had exchanged fear for faith, and we can be her daughters of promise if we will dare to do the same.

> *You are her daughters if you do what is right and do not give way to fear.* (1 Peter 3:6 NIV)

Tamar

In the Bible there is a rather determined and scandalous woman named Tamar. Twice widowed, she would not be denied a child. God killed her first husband because he was wicked and the second because he would not give her a son. (Don't tell me God doesn't protect His girls!) Two dead husbands later, God was still as determined this woman would have legacy proceed from her life. Her father-in-law, Judah, promised his third son to her, and she was sent away to wait until he came of age. And wait she did. She lived as a widow in her father's house, and when the time came for her to be taken again as a wife, she was not summoned. Judah's wife died and Tamar heard of it. Undaunted, she dressed as a prostitute and waited, veiled, by the side of the road. Judah did not recognize her and wanted to lie with her but had no payment. She requested his staff, signet, and cord in pledge for the young goat he promised to send back. Judah lay with her, and she conceived.

Afterward, she laid aside the garments of a harlot and again put on her widow's clothing. When Judah was told she was pregnant by harlotry, he recommended death by burning as her punishment . . . that was, until she sent his staff, signet, and cord.

> *Judah recognized them and said, "She is more righteous than I, since I wouldn't give her to my son."*   (Genesis 38:26 NIV)

Then everything changed. Judah took her as his wife but never touched her again (I personally think he was afraid to). Tamar gave birth to twin sons (for the two she was denied). She and her son Perez are mentioned in the lineage of Christ. Tamar exchanged widowhood and treachery for motherhood and honor.

Rahab

Tamar played the harlot; Rahab actually was a harlot. This woman hid the Israelite spies and covered their escape from Jericho. In return, she made them take an oath to spare her and her entire family. Rahab exchanged the fear of judgment and death for the fear of the Lord. An entire city quaked in terror, but only one, a prostitute, got what was really going on.

> *Our hearts melted and everyone's courage failed because of*
> *you, for the LORD your God is God in heaven above and on*
> *the earth below.* (Joshua 2:11 NIV)

Everyone in Jericho knew this was true. But only Rahab embraced it and did something with this truth. She defied her earthly king and rescued the spies of God's chosen. She was yet another woman who found herself and her descendants (Boaz) in the lineage of Christ. Rahab even made the Hall of Faith.

> *By faith the harlot Rahab did not perish with those who did*
> *not believe, when she had received the spies with peace.*
> (Hebrews 11:31 NKJV)

Deborah

We have dedicated an entire chapter (see chapter 14) to this amazing woman who exchanged merely sitting in judgment for the dynamic of standing in the gap until there was something more.

Ruth and Naomi

Both of these women exchanged death and disappointment for hope and promise. Ruth exchanged the love of herself to care for her mother-in-law and found the love of her life. Naomi poured out a mother's heart and exchanged grief and loss for adoption and legacy.

Hannah

Inevitably, God asks each of us what we will call the dead and barren places of our lives. Will we continue to call them wretched and hopeless? Or will we speak life's hope and promise? Repeatedly, when God's covenant women found themselves barren (Sarah, Rebekah, Rachel, Hannah, and Elizabeth are just a few), it caused them to press in and cry out for something more. They understood their barrenness was not a

| *God births promise.* |

punishment or rejection or denial. The truth is that often through our longing, God births promise.

> *But to Hannah he [her husband] gave a double portion because he loved her, and the LORD had closed her womb. And because the LORD had closed her womb, her rival kept provoking her in order to irritate her.*   (1 Samuel 1:5–6 NIV)

Only God gives life out of barren places. Hannah was just such a woman. She understood she needed something more than what her husband could ever give her. She already had his love and his respect. He honored Hannah by giving her, his barren wife, the double portion at each feast. This was not enough. She longed for something deeper and stronger. A rival wife provoked Hannah in order to discourage her. Instead, this taunting drove Hannah to the temple and into deep prayer.

Eli, an overweight and corrupt priest, saw her and mistakenly believed her to be drunk. But this wise woman knew how to draw a blessing from someone who had just misjudged her. She answered his dishonor with honor. She received her answer and left Eli's presence with a smile on her face. The next time her adversary saw her, she met a very different countenance.

> *I smile at my enemies, because I rejoice in Your salvation.*
>   (1 Samuel 2:1 NKJV)

Hannah exchanged dishonor for honor and offense for victory. She set apart her son even before he was conceived. Her prayer progressed from "Give me a son for my husband's sake," to "Give me a son because I am tormented by an adversary," to ultimately, "God, give me a son, and I will give him back to You." Samuel grew up before the Lord, and God gave her more children to fill her home.

> *And the LORD visited Hannah, so that she conceived and bore*
> *three sons and two daughters. Meanwhile the child Samuel*
> *grew before the LORD.* (1 Samuel 2:21 NKJV)

A formerly barren woman birthed a lineage of prophets.

Abigail

Then there is Abigail. What's a woman to do when it appears the enemy is your own husband? This is a long story because there is so much to glean:

There was a man named Nabal, and his wife, Abigail. She was wise and beautiful, but he was harsh and evil. David and his men were hiding in the wilderness near Nabal's settlement. They guarded his sheep and people by acting as a wall of protection around his property. David sent a few men to ask if they could be part of the shearing festivals. But rather than include them, Nabal reviled them. One of Nabal's young men told Abigail how foolishly her husband had behaved and posed this problem:

> *Now therefore, know and consider what you will do, for*
> *harm is determined against our master and against all his*
> *household.* (1 Samuel 25:17 NKJV)

Save us, Abigail! There is a crisis hanging over us, and our master is too dumb to know it. I love how this woman responded. She wasted no time, but quickly amassed a feast to take to David and his men. She knew this was her only hope of saving her household from certain slaughter. You may wonder how she dared to do this without even consulting her husband. Abigail knew what was in her hand and what was in her power to give. As his wife, she had the power to spend her portion even if her husband refused to share his. She spent her abundance to save the lives of others.

> *Then Abigail made haste and took two hundred loaves of*
> *bread, two skins of wine, five sheep already dressed, five*

seahs of roasted grain, one hundred clusters of raisins, and
two hundred cakes of figs, and loaded them on donkeys. And
she said to her servants, "Go on before me; see, I am coming
after you." But she did not tell her husband Nabal.

(vv. 18–19 NKJV)

When Abigail saw David, she ran to him and fell at his feet. Picture
this: an angry warrior, surrounded by his men, is coming to shed the
blood of every male in the settlement. Perhaps the only thing capable of
distracting him was a beautiful woman running toward him and falling
at his feet.

On me, my lord, on me let this iniquity be! And please let
your maidservant speak in your ears, and hear the words of
your maidservant.   (v. 24 NKJV)

How amazing was this woman . . . she stopped an angry mob and
took the blame as her own. Once she knew she had David's complete attention, she used the power of the softly spoken word. Notice her approach: "Please let your maidservant speak in your ears." What was she
doing? She averted David's sin with a whisper. She counseled him in a
voice far too low for his men to hear. She told him not to even think
about Nabal, who was a fool. She positioned him too low to even merit
David's attention, then she lifted David's eyes to God's promises by ap-
pealing to his sense of godliness. She admonished David to not avenge
himself and then reminded him why:

For the LORD *will certainly make for my lord an enduring*
house, because my lord fights the battles of the LORD, *and*
evil is not found in you throughout your days.   (v. 28 NKJV)

David, don't let evil be found in you now that you are on the verge of
getting it all. This had to be an immense source of encouragement to

David. He'd roamed the wilderness with nothing but God's promises for years while Nabal and King Saul had abundance. I love her words; in them we find a promise for us all. If we fight God's battles, He will uphold our houses and extend our legacies. Neither the house of Nabal nor Saul endured. Nabal died without an heir, and Saul's house was put to the sword and his daughter was childless.

We are not to fight for ourselves. We fight for God and on behalf of others. David kept this standard before him for the rest of his life. He repeatedly refused to use his influence and power to punish those who reviled him. He used his position of strength only to deal with those who reviled the Lord.

> *When the LORD has done for my lord according to all the good that He has spoken concerning you, and has appointed you ruler over Israel, that this will be no grief to you, nor offense of heart to my lord, either that you have shed blood without cause, or that my lord has avenged himself. But when the LORD has dealt well with my lord, then remember your maidservant.* (vv. 30–31 NKJV)

Abigail reminded David of God's word, then asked him to remember her when he found himself positioned in promise. Why would she ask such a thing? She understood that when you position others for promise, you can't help but enjoy the benefit of it yourself.

> *Then David said to Abigail: "Blessed is the LORD God of Israel, who sent you this day to meet me! And blessed is your advice and blessed are you, because you have kept me this day from coming to bloodshed and from avenging myself with my own hand. For indeed, as the LORD God of Israel lives, who has kept me back from hurting you, unless you had hurried and come to meet me, surely by morning light no males would have been left to Nabal!"* (vv. 32–34 NKJV)

Abigail returned home and found her husband drunk. Wisely, she waited until morning to tell him all that had transpired. I imagine he was a bit hungover when he heard her words, but still Scripture says his heart died within him and he turned to stone. Ten days later, God struck him dead. Okay . . . there is a lesson here: Don't mess with those who fight for the Lord!

When David heard about Nabal's death, he asked Abigail to be his wife! Maybe it is wrong for me to say this, but I would much rather be married to David in the wilderness than live with a grump with money.

This wise woman exchanged the foolishness of her husband for the life of her household and counseled a king when her own husband would not listen.

Jael

Jael is perhaps my favorite . . . well, at least she is my favorite to preach about. Jael was another woman whose husband was on the wrong side. He had made an allegiance with the enemy of Israel. She understood that when the enemy comes too near you have to take him out. She did not realize her victory on the bloody fields of battle, but rather within the walls of her tent. She lulled an enemy general asleep, then wielded what she had in her hand—a hammer and a tent peg. He fell asleep under her watch never to wake again. She exchanged ungodly alliances for godly ones.

Bathsheba

This young and beautiful wife found herself in the midst of a scandal when King David saw her and sent for her. She slept with him and became pregnant. David arranged her husband's death and then quickly took her as his wife to cover his deed. But there was no hiding their choices from God. It was not long before the prophet Nathan confronted David, and their firstborn son died. Somehow through it all, the beautiful Bathsheba stayed tender. She conceived again and gave birth to a second son, Solomon. She raised him in the fear of the Lord and taught him to desire wisdom above all else. She exchanged scandal and death for honor, wisdom, legacy, and promise.

Elizabeth

This blameless, barren matriarch exchanged years of disappointment for God's promise. Like Sarah, she received the promise of God and found out that what was impossible for man was possible for God. Even in her pregnancy, she exchanged the admiration of her people for sanctifying seclusion and a fresh infilling of the Holy Spirit. This wise mother spoke prophetically to her spiritual daughter and mother of our Lord, Mary, and transferred this blessing, which remains for each of us today: "Blessed is she who has believed that what the Lord has said to her will be accomplished!" (Luke 1:45 NIV).

Mary

Mary exchanged the uncertainty and shame of being an unwed mother for the surety of God's promise. She exchanged her fears for God's favor. Her words stand as an example for all time: "Let it be to me according to your word" (Luke 1:38 NKJV).

What About Us?

How do we connect with wisdom so we can make these divine exchanges? The following Scriptures show us where to begin:

> *The fear of the* LORD *is the beginning of wisdom; all who follow his precepts have good understanding.* (Psalm 111:10 NIV)

> *The fear of the* LORD *is true wisdom; to forsake evil is real understanding.* (Job 28:28 NLT)

Wisdom is intimately tied to our fear of the Lord, just as understanding is related to our response to evil. What does it mean to fear the Lord? It is to love what He loves (wisdom and justice) and hate what He hates (foolishness and evil). Perhaps you have never invited God to impart His holy fear into your life. This would be key, because without holy fear, wisdom cannot even have a beginning.

When I began my quest to gain wisdom and understanding, I just took the instructions of Proverbs literally. I was traveling as a promotional representative for a major cosmetics firm, and I spent almost forty weeks on the road per year. I would climb into bed each night with my Bible and just do what it said. I confessed my foolish simple ways. I called wisdom my sister. I cried out for understanding.

I asked for the fear of the Lord. Slowly but surely, I began to see its counsel in my life. God's wisdom is so vast and multifaceted.

In Proverbs, we find He is our source and abundant supply:

> For the LORD *gives wisdom; from His mouth come knowledge and understanding; He stores up sound wisdom for the upright.*   (2:6–7 NKJV)

Our heavenly Father stores up wisdom, waiting for us just to ask Him. He longs to pour out wisdom on the hungry and refreshing on those who thirst for more. He promises to accept what we bring Him in exchange. We present our foolishness and lack of answers, and He in return gives us His wisdom, direction, and counsel.

Proverbs 3:13-18 describes how wisdom benefits our entire lives:

> Happy is the person who finds *wisdom and gains understanding. For the profit of wisdom is better than silver, and* her *wages are better than gold. Wisdom is more precious than rubies; nothing you desire can compare with* her. She *offers you life in* her *right hand, and riches and honor in* her *left. She will guide you down delightful paths; all* her *ways are satisfying. Wisdom is a tree of life to those who embrace* her; *happy are those who hold* her *tightly.*   (NLT, emphasis added)

An entire book could not cover the wonder and beauty of God's wisdom. She is a precious treasure each of us can pursue. I am so thankful that you do not have to be extremely bright or highly educated in order to be wise. According to the book of James, God gives wisdom to all who will simply ask Him:

> *If you need wisdom—if you want to know what God wants you to do—ask him, and he will gladly tell you. He will not resent your asking. But when you ask him, be sure that you really expect him to answer, for a doubtful mind is as unsettled as a wave of the sea that is driven and tossed by the wind.*
>
> (1:5–6 NLT)

Let's ask God for this treasure and be sensitive to any exchanges we need to make.

Heavenly Father,

This day I turn my ear to wisdom and apply my heart to understanding. I want to be a woman who personifies wisdom here on earth. I call wisdom my sister and confidante. Open my ears and heart to receive Your insight and instruction. Right now, by the power of Your Holy Spirit, show me the exchanges I need to make. I want to lay hold of life and Your Word and let go of all that would lead to death and deception. I release bitterness, unforgiveness, anger, pain, fear, jealousy, hatred, turmoil, and disappointments from my past.

Shed Your light of truth in my inmost parts. I choose to wisely spend my life. I want to walk wisdom's paths and not follow the way of foolishness. Anoint me with wisdom's riches and honor, and let me become like a tree of life to all who embrace me. I know for any of this to begin, I will need an impartation of the holy fear of the Lord. Father God, fill me with Your holy fear now by the power of Your Holy Spirit. I choose to shun evil and embrace understanding. Amen.

CHAPTER EIGHT

Wielding Favor and Glory

We have been awakened to the power of our influence and our feminine ability to elevate many aspects of earthly life. Now the question arises, how do we effectively appropriate our gifts to a world so desperate for their impact? In this chapter I want to address more specifically how women bestow or confer the gift of honor. I believe a powerful exchange happens when women extend this unique and particular contribution. Perhaps you didn't know you had such a treasure to transfer. It is a gift that gives back to the one who bestows. Perhaps you did not realize you are referred to as both "favor" and "the glory of man." First, the glory issue:

> *The woman is the glory of man.*   (1 Corinthians 11:7 NIV)

To be referenced as "the glory" is the ultimate of compliments. Here it describes a *relational* dynamic. It is more than a declaration of value; it lends clarification of our unique reflective role. Just as the man reflects strength, the woman reflects beauty in its many forms. Before there is even a chance of anyone getting a bit of attitude, let's review this in the light of two truths: (1) Women are an answer, not a problem, and (2) the description of woman as the man's glory was never meant to demean or belittle her role or feminine contribution. It was meant to uplift by assigning value and honor.

We should look at the Word of God through the light of redemption and restoration rather than through the distortion and destruction of the Fall. So what is glory? Glory denotes magnificence, splendor, beauty, and wonder. Women accurately represent this reflection in the male-female relational dynamic. Glory is further described as beauty that inspires feelings of wonder and joy. Doesn't this perfectly describe Adam's initial reaction to Eve? He was awestruck by all she awoke in him. She was the reflection and image of all he'd longed for but had yet to see in his surroundings or himself.

So why have we used God's Word, which describes a beautiful relational dynamic, to reduce and label women as inferior to men? As previously addressed, there is an evil one who does not want men and women to function in healthy complementary roles. He knows if we realize the truth, he can no longer divide us. He wants the conflict between us to remain so we will continue to wrestle each other for power and position. It is once again the irreconcilable hostility of a serpent spreading his overarching static in an attempt to distort what we hear. Echoing this static robs the richness and beauty of truth. All truth ultimately brings freedom. If men and women can get this right and learn how to complement and complete each other, then everyone and everything under their dominion will be benefited.

> *For man was not [created] from the woman, but woman from man; neither was man created on account of or for the benefit of woman, but woman on account of and for the benefit of man.* (1 Corinthians 11:8–9 AMP)

This reiterates the need men have for women. We add value and meaning to every aspect of their lives. Women are created in the *image* of God,

> *The man was made from dirt, and the woman was wonderfully made for a garden.*

but bear a glory different from that reflected by men. Men and women are equal, but not interchangeable. We do not hold the position of first created, but we hold the honor of being the crowning finale. The man was made from dirt, and the woman was wonderfully made for a garden.

The Bible never said it was wrong for the woman to be alone, only that it was *not good* for the man to be by himself. Eve was his helpmeet, the one who made up for all he lacked. Never doubt the value and importance of this role. I remember when John asked me to marry him, it was almost as though he were presenting me with a job description. Here is my call in life. This is what I'll be doing; do you want to help me do it? I was stunned. Was that it? Had I just won best applicant? Where were the passion and the romance? John told me I did not have to answer him right then, so I didn't. That night I cried. God, what is this? I heard the Spirit whisper, *You are the desire of John's heart.* I thought, *I just don't see that in the way he is acting.* Oh, but I was blind. He loved me desperately; he just didn't know how to say it. Now, after nearly twenty-five years of marriage, he still lights up when he sees me. Why? I am his glory.

Is Man's Glory Greater Than Woman's?

Do we get bent out of shape when we hear man referred to as the glory of God in 1 Corinthians 11:7?

> *He is the image and glory of God.*   (NIV)

Does God use the strength of this relationship to dominate males? No, it is simply a relational dynamic and a constant point of rejoicing for God. He looks at His magnificent creation, man, and smiles! And yes, when He glances at you, daughter, He is captivated. Likewise, when the man beholds the magnificence of the woman, he is enraptured. Does love dominate its beloved? Only the foolish man forgets she is likened to a crown about his head. When referring to the glory, there are two dynamics found in the Scriptures. First, there is the glory of mankind and how we relate to God. Second, there is the relational glory between the man and the woman. The psalmist David wondered at this relationship between God and His glory, mankind, when he posed this question:

> *What is man that you are mindful of him?* (Psalm 8:4 NIV)

In the next verse, David answered his own question and established both order and honor:

> *You made him a little lower than the heavenly beings and crowned him with glory and honor.* (v. 5 NIV)

As he pondered the wonder of creation, David was overwhelmed and awed by God's response to us. That He would crown the breath-filled dirt of mankind with glory and honor seemed unfathomable to this worshiping king. Mankind collectively reflects God's glory and honor. Likewise, woman is crowned as this reflection of the man. Without going into a major theological dissertation, I believe this means at least in part that the woman has the power to reflect all the man would hope or aspire to be. A woman's presence often adds meaning and purpose to a man's life and labor. The Scripture also spells out both the danger and folly of men's and women's dishonoring of what God has set apart for honor. The book of James describes this conflict in the body:

> *With the tongue we praise our Lord and Father, and with it we curse men, who have been made in God's likeness.* (3:9 NIV)

We are to bless God as well as bless what He blesses. If we are the crown of God's creation, then why would we ever seek to dishonor and dominate each other? Wouldn't this actually be working against God's purposes for men and women? When men do not love and nurture women, they hurt themselves (see Ephesians 5:28-29). In the same way, if women do not honor and respect men, they ultimately dishonor themselves. I don't know about you, but I certainly don't want to find myself at odds with or in opposition to God. I want to align myself with His purposes. I want to build up and never destroy His sons and daughters. I want to strengthen both men and women.

The Way Women Ignite Vision

There is something amazing that happens when a woman lends her affinity for relational intimacy to the physical strength of the man. Her gift of feminine intuition and insight has the ability to see him not as he is, but as who he could be. This interchange awakens a dormant desire within the man. He longs to be the man she envisions. This often catches him unaware. Is he mistaken, or did he catch a glimpse of his altered likeness in the eyes of his beloved wife, mother, sister, or daughter? When he looks into the woman's eyes, he sees himself as he could be, or should be if love would have its way. God stirs the heart of the brother, the father, the son, or the bridegroom. It is the awakening again of Adam to Eve. He wants the chance to prove himself true.

We have some friends who had three sons, and then they were blessed with the gift of a beautiful baby girl. As she grew, her father's life expanded. He shared how his daughter had awakened a protective and tender side of him, which had never been quickened fathering sons.

In my childhood, my father was often harsh and abrupt with my mother and brother. There was a chair he always sat in, watching TV or reading his paper while he smoked. It was as though he had a barrier around him that said, "I am here, but I am not engaged." Countless times I would approach the ominous chair and climb into the lap of my father. He would grunt and grumble as I laid my head against his chest, feigning interest in his paper or program. Sometimes I was just quiet. It wasn't long before I would sense him relax, and his mood would soften a bit. As though to say, "Yes, I needed that, but I did not know it." If he had come home from work exhausted, I was always the one sent to call him for dinner. Mine was the only voice he would not grumble back at when awakened from his sleep.

The Call of Tenderness

There is a tenderness that calls to something more in a man. He wants to be gentle enough to handle the piece of crystal because he understands it is both valuable and sensitive.

This is very different from how I had tried to mold John. I wanted him to conform to the image I had of him, rather than nurture the reflection he caught of himself. In the realm of marriage, a union and alliance is formed from which life and love can proceed. In a father, the desire to nurture and protect is quickened. In a son, the hope of honoring his mother and father is stirred. In a brother, the desire to protect and understand his sister and her feminine responses is realized.

To visually illustrate this, I want you to imagine a beautiful maiden extending a sword in the gesture of knighting a young man who kneels before her. He goes down a man and arises a knight. What interchange has just taken place? Why does this man kneel before her?

The woman has transferred something intangible to the young man bowed before her. He kneels because she embodies the very reason and hope for his pledge. He vows to protect all she represents with the edge of his sword and the strength of his might. If war, peril, or great need were to arise, he would count his life forfeit if it meant protecting hers. He has pledged his honor to preserve a nobler way of life, to defend their country as well as her honor and virtue. I love this image. It conveys the power of feminine virtue and beauty to stir a man to a higher purpose. It is the gentle awakening the strong by bestowing glory.

He does not fear the sword when it is in her hand. In her possession, it is no longer a weapon but an instrument of transformation. It is not presented to threaten, wound, or strike the man; it is extended to set him apart. He is no longer the same. As a knight, his life has been expanded and his name enlarged to encompass a title and eventually a legacy. He has been dubbed and elevated. This means both weight and honor have been added to his name. With the sword, she transfers power and confers something only she can give: a higher purpose and reason to live.

He does not experience the edge of the sword when it is in her hands. He feels the sword's full weight as the flat of it is transferred from shoulder to shoulder. With this solemn act, she grants him the necessary authority and entitlement. He now shoulders the responsibility and honor of the one who bears the sword.

A Walk Worthy of the Sword

Knights were entrusted with the privilege of bearing the sword only after pledging themselves to honor and conduct as outlined in the Code of Chivalry. This code specified how justice was to be upheld. It was a pledge to protect both the kingdom and all who were sheltered within its borders. With the sword at his side, the knight represented the authority and might of the king. He served his king by protecting the subjects of the kingdom from injustice and lawlessness. It was of utmost importance that he wield it faithfully, because in the knight's hand the sword and the authority behind it could not be separated. This is not merely a feudal dynamic; it is a kingdom principle. This is why an oath or a pledge had to be secured to be certain the knight would not misrepresent or abuse the authority of the sword.

> *For he is God's servant to do you good. But if you do wrong, be afraid, for he does not bear the sword for nothing. He is God's servant, an agent of wrath to bring punishment on the wrongdoer.*   (Romans 13:4 NIV)

But alas, no matter the precautions, there are always mercenaries and renegades who carry a sword, though not all have proved themselves worthy to wield it. They have not submitted to a code of ethics, let alone the Word of God. They bear no true authority or title because they have not submitted themselves to truth, but instead live under the banner of self and their own ambitions. They do not understand loyalty or patriotism, because such sentiments require submission to a king or a code. To them, rebellion is freedom and submission bondage. They took the easy route and purchased what should have been awarded.

There is yet another sword that cannot be purchased, for it is alive.

The Living Sword

The word of God is living and active. Sharper than any double-edged sword, it penetrates even to dividing soul and spirit, joints and marrow; it judges the thoughts and attitudes of the heart. (Hebrews 4:12 NIV)

Men and women alike are entrusted with this gift, "the sword of the Spirit, which is the word of God" (Ephesians 6:17 NLT). Not only is it a powerful weapon; it has the ability to reveal our thoughts and attitudes as well. In the kingdom of God, everything is ultimately measured by motivation (see 1 Corinthians 13). How we submit or react to the truth of God's Word or sword often reveals our motives. In the kingdom of God, it is wisdom that knights or empowers the sons and daughters of God.

> *If any of you lacks wisdom, he should ask God, who gives generously to all without finding fault, and it will be given to him.* (James 1:5 NIV)

Wisdom is how we appropriately utilize our words and the Word of God. It is freely available to all who will ask in faith. Those who truly have authority are under wisdom's authority. They understand that the ultimate power comes to those under God's divine rule. As we submit to the tenets of His Word, we find ourselves protected. The sword watches over all who take shelter under its care. Conversely, if we do not submit to the sword of His Word, we will soon find the sword set against us. There are those who use the Word of God to serve themselves rather than to further God's kingdom. They wield the sword of God's Word as a legalistic letter that destroys the spirit and wounds the soul.

> *For the letter kills, but the Spirit gives life.*
> (2 Corinthians 3:6 NIV)

A sword can cut both ways. Too often I have seen the sword of God's Word mishandled when it comes to male-female relationships. Either men are elevated at the expense of women, or men are displaced by the anger and frustration of women. You hear it in phrases such as "Women, get back in your place!" and "Men, it's our turn now!" When the sword is faithfully handled, it will always bring about justice and the preservation of life. But when the law is executed without the heart of the King or His Spirit, it brings death to the subjects of the kingdom. When the Word of God pertaining to gender roles has been taught to women, it often has been from the letter, rather than from a life-giving Spirit frame of reference. We've interpreted the Scriptures as commands to regulate the behavior of problematic women rather than as directives on how men and women are to relate to each other.

> *In the LORD, however, woman is not independent of man, nor is man independent of woman. For as woman came from man, so also man is born of woman. But everything comes from God.*   (1 Corinthians 11:11–12 NIV)

Note the preface, "In the Lord." This settles everything. In Him, men and women are dependent on and connected with each other. Why? It is because both male and female have their origins in God. The man and the woman are to be complementary and interdependent. In God's eyes, the woman is not only the man's glory; she is his favor with God.

> *The man who finds a wife finds a treasure and receives favor from the* LORD. (Proverbs 18:22 NLT)

God's Favor for His Daughters

Both treasure and favor are undeniable assets. God is amazing, for even now He is taking the sword of His Word and turning things around for His daughters. The very sword that has been at times used against us will soon battle on our behalf.

> *The* LORD *executes righteousness and justice for all who are oppressed.* (Psalm 103:6 NKJV)

The daughters of God are destined for justice. Judgment represents a decision for or against. God alone is the One who can rightly administer true justice. Where there have been oppression and fear, there will be an even greater release as the Lord begins to execute righteousness. He is carrying out His decree of everlasting love and restoring the correct order and position of honor for His sons and daughters. We are seeing men and women the world over joining their strengths for the benefit of one another rather than wielding their power against one another.

Should we behave according to how we have been treated or in accordance with righteousness? Should we dishonor others because we ourselves have been dishonored? No, now is the time to give it all to God. As women, it is our season to transfer honor and title. No one can take this privilege away, for we are of the royal lineage of the daughters of Sarah. We are destined to crown Jesus with the honor only we can bestow upon Him as our beloved King. He has given us His royal name, and we are simply bestowing the honor of the victory He has already won. Women have been entrusted with the privilege of adorning the body as a bride in preparation for our Lord's return.

Look around you. Authentic women are arising the world over, declaring His love and truth and recovering their former glory. I am an answer. I am wise and beautiful. I have favor and honor to bestow. I am a daughter of the Most High God, who inspires awe and wonder.

———————

Heavenly Father,

I come to You in the name of Jesus, thanking You for both the privilege and the honor of the designation of favor and glory. I want to bring Your favor to every life I touch. I want to reflect Your beauty, awe, and wonder. I want to release the splendor of heaven here on earth. I will extend the sword of the Word of God to transfer honor and title. I will speak and awaken the noble in the common. I will elevate Your plans and purpose as the knowledge of Your glory fills this earth as the waters cover the seas. Now raise and empower me, your royal daughter, in Jesus' name. Amen.

———————

CHAPTER NINE

What Is the Power of Love?

Movies have become a common language and love stories a favorite theme. Films are quite possibly the only medium with power to move this jaded world by awakening senses long dulled by years of disappointment and overstimulation. God is not afraid of this medium. He is more than happy to move through this multisensory approach to draw His children to Himself.

Under a film's influence, the human heart can be temporarily captivated and transported to a realm beyond the reach and impact of the outside world. Movies speak directly to the mind in the fluent language of the heart. This type of interchange happens regardless of whether the message relayed is for our benefit or detriment. Movies have the power to exploit our deepest fears or quicken dreams long dead.

God can use this melding of story, beautiful cinematography, and powerful music to punctuate and expound truth. We would be foolish indeed if we did not listen to our culture's cry for hope, love, and goodness. It is possible for all three to speak to us in a movie's story line and imagery, which often communicate a longing so large and painful it could not be captured or conveyed in the language of words alone.

We realize this concept is not new when we understand that each life is a story. Every scene is recorded in a heavenly book. God has woven you into His beautiful epic. This makes the issue about so much more than a woman, a culture, or Christianity . . . it becomes a matter of purpose and intent.

> *Your eyes saw my unformed body. All the days ordained for*
> *me were written in your book before one of them came to be.*
>   (Psalm 139:16 NIV)

We Determine What Stories Our Lives Tell

Daughter, what story do you want to tell? Mother, what legacy would you leave behind for your children? Beloved, what is your love story? My children have something more in them. I catch it in the faraway glimpses of their eyes. I hear its voice in the music that moves them. I want my life to speak to them in a way they can understand. Love alone crosses all boundaries of time.

Though we cannot determine how our stories begin, we are very much a part of how they will end. Never doubt, there is a wrestling match taking place for how your tale will close. More often than not, happy endings come only after there has been a battle waged with evil. In our world, very little good happens without some sort of fight. Each and every day could be likened to a page. We are the writers who craft the stories with our words and choices. This is but one of the reasons why stories speak so powerfully to us.

When Jesus walked the earth as a man, He was a master storyteller. He packaged timeless messages in word pictures. He used parables, natural law, and real-life experiences to teach His audiences about His Father's kingdom. He wanted the truth to be heard within the framework of living, progressive pictures. He took the abstract and made it tangible and embraceable in the everyday.

We could almost say stories are the original form of movies, be-cause as plots develop, we find our minds moving from one scene to the next. We do not merely hear or read stories; we see them as only we can. In the secret places of our hearts and minds, they take form. Within the framework of our imaginations, characters are cast with whom only we can identify. They move freely and fill in the blanks as the story unfolds.

So what about your story? Before the most exciting parts of your story can be realized, you must first discover your role. I am afraid far too often a true casting never happens. We float through life, hoping someone else will tell us what parts we are to play. There is great potential for danger when we make others responsible for our hap-piness. God is the ultimate storyteller who wants to reveal His love story in you. He has written your role and scripted the desires of your heart.

Love Declared; Interdependence Revealed

I recently watched a poignant love story called *The Village*. I found it to be a brilliant wealth of unspeakable loveliness and longing set in an unreal almost-dream world. If you have not seen it for fear it is a horror movie, I can assure you, it is not. It is both wholesome and thought-provoking, and one movie I would highly recommend. To my best abil-ity I will recount a few of the scenes for you, which I believe capture the essence of love and legacy.

The scene: It is late. Ivy, a vivacious blind girl, discovers Lucius sitting on her porch. The night is well spent, and a mist is rising. He has come to protect her, to keep vigil as she sleeps during the last watch of the night. Slipping outside, she joins him. She teases him, asking why he is on *her* porch rather than on another in the village. She chides him in an attempt to get him to declare his affection for her. When this doesn't work, she tries another tactic: "Do you find me too much of a tomboy? I do long to do boy things . . . It's so exciting."

He offers no comment, so she continues, "How is it that you are brave when all the rest of us shake in our boots?"

He answers with an air of nonchalance, "I do not worry about what will happen, only about what needs to be done."

Impressed, she pauses a moment, then continues, "When we are married . . . will you dance with me? I find dancing very agreeable."

He is silent. She knows he loves her, yet he will not speak of it. When her question goes unanswered, she impatiently adds, "Why can you not say what is in your head?"

His response is one of frustration. "Why can you not stop saying what is in yours? Why must you lead when I want to lead? If I want to dance, I will ask you to dance. If I want to speak, I will open my mouth and speak . . . What good is it to tell you that you are in my every thought from the time I wake? What good can come of my saying that I sometimes cannot think clearly or do my work properly? What gain can rise from my telling you that the only time I feel fear as others do is when I think of you in harm? That is why I am on this porch, Ivy Walker! I fear for your safety before all others. And yes, I will dance with you on our wedding night."

A quiet settles over them both. She trembles like a leaf overcome by the intensity of his outburst. In the aftermath of this passionate revelation, a tear falls. Everything has changed because love has been openly declared. Now neither of them can find their way back without the other. He reaches over and gently kisses her.

For Ivy, the leap has been made. No longer does she desire to be one of the guys. She has realized this portion of herself in the man before her. Her feminine life will be mingled with his in a way no other man could be joined with him. She has found her protector and he his beloved. She is the reason behind all he does. In a moment's time, the two have become one heart. Their strengths have met and found a place of rest in the presence of each other. Equally matched, they fit perfectly together. As I watched this interchange, tears traced my cheeks.

Strength Calls Forth Strength

There is such beauty when strength gives place to strength. It is where our weaknesses are compensated and our assets maximized. A woman does not yield to a man because she is weak; she yields because she has found the place, that safe place in which to entrust her dreams, to lend her strengths and find her vulnerabilities protected. It is something reflected in the eyes of the one to whom she will choose to open her life and with whom she will bear joy, children, and sorrows. He is the vessel into which she can pour her love and life. All the good stored up in her can be safely released to him. Why? He would give his life to preserve hers.

In this scene, Lucius revealed she was his one weakness. With this revelation, Ivy is positioned to freely give him her strength. If she had been a different kind of woman, she might have used his need against him. If she had access to modern counsel, she might have exploited his longing and fears for her own purpose and protection. She could have chosen to manipulate him. Before you are ever tempted to choose this route, know that in games of manipulation, both sides eventually suffer loss. The woman loses her power of influence, and the man loses a safe place to entrust his heart.

Our need for each other was never meant to be a weakness to be exploited, but a dynamic to be celebrated. We all long for such a place of safety and intimacy. What is it that we protect? Do we safeguard our places of strength or our vulnerabilities? Anyone who abuses his source of protection is a fool. Women are vulnerable in the area of physical strength, and men often find their hearts at risk. We

> *Women, is there any commission more noble than to be the guardian of a heart?*

women are the caretakers of men's hearts, just as surely as the men should be the protectors and providers for any physical weakness in us. Women, is there any commission more noble than to be the guardian of a heart?

Was it not Adam who declared Eve to be just what he needed? Eve did not say this when she saw Adam. From the beginning, did not the man long for the unique help of the woman? He did not need her help in his labor so much as he needed her as a companion of the heart. He was alone without one who was like him and yet different enough to encompass his vulnerable heart.

Stay Open to Love

Everything of value in this life carries with it some form of risk. There is the threat of losing control and the curse of failure, but there is no fear in love. Why? Love can never fail. Therefore, when love is found, it should be protected at all cost. It should be the driving force behind all we do. Once we have love, it cannot be separated from us without causing great injury. I realize that I am painting a picture of what should be rather than what often is. But in this picture, I believe you will glimpse the power of what could be and move from the domain of disappointment to the realm of hope.

Once love is openly declared, there is no going back. This happens between a man and a woman as well as between Christ and His beloved bride. For with Him, there is no coming back from the promise of the love that propelled Him to risk it all. I know men in their many frail and human forms of father, brother, boyfriend, and husband may have disappointed you, but God cannot. It is not possible for Him to fail you. Men love, but God *is* Love.

If we are to move beyond survival in our human relationships, we must allow our hearts to remain open to the transforming power of love.

Once Ivy learned of Lucius's desperate *longing for her,* she never again *desired to be him*. He was not drawn to her by the ways she was like him; he embraced her for the strengths she awakened within him. Though she was once complete alone, she now refused to be without him.

Do we women seek to be men because we long for what they alone can bring to our lives? In our desperation, have we forgotten that by becoming their piece of the puzzle, we have lost the intimate fit?

While we were so busy coaching them on how to be men, did we forget what it was to be women?

Are we afraid they will so profoundly fail us that we will not entrust them with the gifts of our love and strength? What can we ever hope to gain by withholding what we were made to give so freely? Must we rob them of their words and take control merely because we are afraid that if we are not speaking we will not be heard? Are we still so frightened that we seek to control so we will not again be hurt?

Return again with me to the story:

Lucius is critically wounded, and there is a desperate need for help from outside the borders of their village. This help might come at great cost to the safety and existence of the whole community. To minimize this risk, only one person may go and bring back what is necessary. Ivy comes to plead her case before her father.

"I am in love."

"I know."

"He is in love with me."

"I know."

"If he dies, all that is left to me will die with him . . . I ask permission to travel—to retrieve help. You are my father. I will listen to you in all things. I will trust your decision."

Though she is desperate and determined, there is no manipulation or threat found in her words. Her words speak the truth encased in the timeless dynamics of love, relationship, trust, obedience, and honor. How could she ever be denied an entreaty so pure, so persuasive?

Ivy's father sees the truth for what it is. Yes, the life of his daughter is entwined with the life of this wounded son. But even more than Lucius's life is at risk. Ivy's plea of "all that is left to me" describes something we often miss in our selfish *now* culture. She is her father's legacy, and it is only through the power of love that he will live on. Why? Without love, nothing of true value can continue.

If I . . . have not love, I am nothing. (1 Corinthians 13:2 NIV)

We can pass on many things to our heirs, but without the motive and preservation of love, they all eventually become nothing. Sex without love becomes nothing. Money without love becomes nothing. Relationships without love are shallow and ultimately lonely. Love transfers legacy as surely as it creates life. Fear is the enemy of love as certainly as love has the power to overcome and displace fear.

> *There is no fear in love; but perfect love casts out fear.*
>   (1 John 4:18 NKJV)

Be Led by Love

Ivy's father sends her on her way and gathers the village elders to tell them what he has done. An argument arises . . . how could he have risked so much to save the love of two? Her father vehemently justifies the choice he made: "Do you plan to live forever? It is in them our future lies . . . Yes, I have risked. I hope I am always able to risk everything for the just and right cause."

Then the question arises, why her? Why send Ivy when she is blind?

"How could you have sent her? She's blind."

"She is led by love. The world moves for love; it kneels before it in awe."

Oh, that we would know and walk in this truth. It is when we learn to love fearlessly that we will find ourselves loved perfectly. Don't be afraid of my words. Those around you may not magically change, but you will. You will be free again. The world trembles before the woman who chooses to fearlessly love. Love is not only one of the weapons and forces women fight with; love is their domain to protect. Like the Word of God, it is both our sword and our promise.

> *The world trembles before the woman who chooses to fearlessly love.*

Take a moment and ask yourself why you might find it hard to give your heart fully to a man.

I know I was afraid that if I loved my husband completely and he left me, I would never recover. This was evident early in our marriage. I was always the first to pull away when we embraced. I discounted his promise of commitment and reasoned that all men leave . . . someday.

John paid for years because of the pain in my past. I remember he once asked, "When will you finally believe me when I say I love you? How old will we have to be before we can actually relax and enjoy our life together . . . seventy? I am willing to wait, but I just think we are missing so much between now and then."

His question riveted me. Would I risk loss and failure to experience love? Or would I continue in my boundaries, always holding back a portion just in case?

I believe you want that place of rest. We can love others because Christ first loved us. Let's surrender to the power of love and let it remove all fear from our relationships.

Building Others

As guardians of the heart, women have the amazing power to strengthen and encourage others. As we extend this gift, we cannot help but be raised ourselves. How does this happen? We lift others by speaking strength to their weaknesses. I am not asking you to embrace denial or ignore the flaws or weaknesses you see. I am just asking you to not engage them in conversation. Rather than conversing about what is wrong, I am challenging you to take your gift of words and strengthen the weak places. It is time to speak the answer rather than the problem. Most people know where they are weak but long to hear the elaboration of where they are strong. Is this not what God does for us? He surrounds us with words of hope, life, promise, and restoration. What is He doing? He is modeling the power of rebuilding lives.

Those from among you shall build the old waste places; you
shall raise up the foundations of many generations; and you

> *shall be called the Repairer of the Breach, the Restorer of*
> *Streets to Dwell In.*   (Isaiah 58:12 NKJV)

There are yet those among us who refuse to believe devastation is our destiny. You are a daughter poised with the power to build, raise, and restore. You can be an answer to the gaping breaches and restore the paths that once again connect those who dwell in our world.

Proverbs chapter 14 opens with this admonition:

> *The wise woman builds her house, but the foolish pulls it*
> *down with her hands.*   (v. 1 NKJV)

There is contrast evident here: we can build with our words or tear down with our hands. Hands represent what we do in our natural abilities. This would include criticism and nagging. Wise women understand that death and life are released through the power of the tongue, and therefore they choose their words wisely. Men and women often need to be affirmed in different ways and areas. Women want to be loved and understood, while men need to be respected and admired.

Regardless of our gender, I can assure you that criticism will ultimately work against your purpose. Though I travel and speak to women, my home-court dynamic is decidedly male. I am the lone female in a home of five men. It is very insightful, living with so much testosterone. Believe me, it is not just women who are hurt by harsh words.

Criticism bites like a sword's edge. It slashes indiscriminately with its stinging judgment, wounding the human heart and squelching the spirit. Proverbs 12:18 says, "Reckless words pierce like a sword" (NIV). If criticism and judgment represent the sword's edge, then surely kindness could be likened to the flat or face of the sword that elevates by lending inspiration and strength. Because we are created in the image of God, He entrusted us with the gift of words. His Word is the ultimate, most powerful sword, but our words can wreak havoc and damage if they are not wielded in love. The book of Proverbs describes a woman's power to knight or build others this way:

> *She opens her mouth with wisdom, and on her tongue is the*
> *law of kindness.*   (31:26 NKJV)

There is more in this verse than might initially be perceived. First, wisdom should be what beckons us to speak. Wisdom always raises others with images of a better way. Women are endowed with both intuition and insight, which give us the awareness of something on a perceptive, intuitive level without actual evidence of its existence—a glimpse into the realm of the unseen and possible. No one can see potential in a man's life like a woman. There is no one better positioned than a mother to speak constant life and nourishment over her sons and

> *No one can see potential in a man's life like a woman.*

daughters, just as there is nothing more healing than to feel simply understood by another woman who knows your weaknesses and yet encourages your strengths.

But our power to influence has the potential to reach even further. Wise women are a gift to their culture. When a woman fosters beauty in and through her life and home, practices discretion, heeds godly instruction, and bestows wisdom, there is no greater source of inspiration. Why do you think voyager ships brandished figures of women at their bows? Was it not an image of both feminine beauty and strength that spurred them on through tempest and danger? Why are all vessels of passage referred to in the feminine? Perhaps it is the feminine presence that calls them ultimately home. Women coax the atmosphere of a home out of the physical structure of a house by filling it with love and nurture.

Women are soft answers that turn away great wrath. The single mothers who know how to press in for the crumbs and see their daughters healed. The competent businesswomen who execute profitable training. They are firm yet gentle. A still, small voice in the midst of a storm. They are the gentle lullaby in a dark and restless night.

When the Power for Good Goes Bad

If we have the power to build, comfort, and heal hearts because we access them at a deeper and more intimate level, then it stands to reason our careless words can do great damage.

"Mommy, please don't let her come over," my son whispered as I tucked him back into bed. John and I had gone out on a rare and wonderful date, and it was after 10:00 p.m. when we returned home. It was a school night, so we were surprised to see our youngest shuffling down the stairs to greet us. He had obviously waited up, listening intently for the garage door. He hugged us both, then asked me to bandage some bug bites he'd managed to scratch into open wounds. I pulled out the Band-Aids and went to work. I sensed he was troubled, but I thought he just wanted some attention before bed. By this time all my sons were out of bed, and John was shooing them back upstairs, but Arden lingered.

"Mommy, will you come up and kiss me?"

"Yes, I will be up in a few minutes," I assured him.

I found him barricaded behind a wall of pillows on his top bunk. I could not see him, but his voice reached down to me.

"Mommy, please don't have her over." I climbed the ladder.

"Arden, who are you talking about? What happened?" I probed.

He mentioned a little girl we knew.

"She said something *really* mean to me," he continued.

Now his older brother Alec on the bottom bunk was listening and chimed in, "What did she say?"

He was hesitant, almost ashamed to repeat her words: "She said she hated me. She said, 'Arden, I hate you!'"

Now, mind you, having three older brothers, my son has been called names before. But this was different. It was the utter and complete rejection of him as a person, and he knew it. Her words had sliced to his very core. I doubt she even realized they'd penetrated so deeply.

"Arden, I am sure she didn't mean it. Sometimes when girls are angry, they say things they don't really mean."

He looked doubtful. I continued, "Well, I am sure she didn't mean to hurt you. Let's pray and forgive her."

As I walked down the stairs, I wondered why it had hurt him so profoundly. As I reflected on it, I truly believed he was wounded by the intensity of her emotion. Even though the offense had occurred outside our home, he wanted my assurance that the offense would not be repeated under our roof. Truly, there is nothing more frightening than feeling unsafe in your own home.

Women's Power to Wound

I thought again of the differences between boys and girls. I believe women are more intimately connected at many levels with their emotions. This is often a vulnerability with men, who are not as emotionally wired as women. This would mean we women have the capacity to wound men like no other because we have the ability to access an intimate target . . . the heart. I have to be honest—in the story of my life, I have been disappointed in men, but I have been wounded by women.

Let's revisit elementary school. Boys might have shoved you on the playground in an attempt to see what you were made of. If you shoved back, or got up or recovered without crying, you earned a measure of acceptance and respect. On the playground, the boys were processing and establishing relationships *physically*. This explains the elaborate array of sports and demonstrations of burgeoning testosterone. The playground approach for girls was quite different. The girls clustered in twos or small, intimate whispering groups to bare their secrets and souls. You were either included or excluded. They might not shove, but you would be given the cold shoulder or the hair flip as they turned from your attempts to connect. As boys celebrated a lack of tears, conversely it seemed the girls *wanted* you to cry.

I almost have to wonder if this is our response to a society that for far too long has not valued or fostered in their daughters what is beautiful, nurturing, wise, and gentle. To survive without inherent gender value, have we evolved and adapted by developing some rather vicious survival skills? If we can't beat up the guys on a physical level, do we attack them from our position of emotional and relational strength? Is this what it means to fight the battle of the sexes? One gender foolishly using their strengths to attack the other where it is the most vulnerable? And what are we fighting to win?

More often than not, women are better communicators of emotion and feeling than men. This should mean we are better at fostering relationships for the benefit of everyone. Most infant girls speak (and potty train) long before their male counterparts. Not only do girls form words earlier, but most are capable of complete sentences while the boys are content to continue communicating with gestures and grunting.

I will never forget the first time I saw this illustrated. While watching my friend's daughter one day, I seated her and my son (who was six months older) side by side in high chairs to feed them. The girl gingerly picked up individual peas with her thumb and forefinger and delicately put them in her mouth. My son, on the other hand, smashed the peas with his hand and then attempted to shove his fist into his mouth. I looked on in shock and proclaimed there was an undeniable difference.

Since in this game of life women and men are intended to be teammates rather than opponents, we need to share our strengths. Instead of criticizing men for what they cannot express, we need to tenderly speak it for them. Rather than pointing out their weaknesses, we should lend them our strengths. Let them smash and we will elegantly applaud their victory.

Case in point: I have had the privilege of editing the majority of my husband's books. At first I felt rather smug about it. I repeatedly pointed out his flaws as I critiqued my way through the chapters. I imagined I was helpful and equipping him for his future writing endeavors, but I was not. I was shaking his confidence and elevating my own personal style.

Finally, I got it. My place was not to criticize his work, but to lend my strength to it. With this revelation, I began to work with a different attitude. Rather than point out all the places I thought he was missing it, I listened for the heart of what he was saying. I presented the chapters I had finished reworking and left the room for him to read alone. Before this, I used to watch over his shoulder so I could point out the wonder of my handiwork. This time he emerged from his study beaming. "You said it just how I wanted to say it!"

He was so excited that I'd understood what he wanted to say and reworked his wording so it could best be heard. He had entrusted me with a weakness, "I know what I want to say, but I am just not sure how to say it," and I gave it back to him with my strength. He felt built up and encouraged. I had caught his heart and communicated it without compromise.

You are a guardian of God's heart. You are an ambassador of His love to a wounded, dying world. Rather than be competitive with others, can we glimpse their hearts and awaken their strengths? Men and women alike are watching and waiting to see the power of His love in your life. What are some of the ways you can speak to weakness and make others strong? What might that look like:

> In the life of your husband?
> In the lives of your children and family?
> In the lives of your friends?
> What about your life? Will you allow love to speak to you and lift you to your position of strength? Commit to say about yourself what God says about you:
> I have loved you with an everlasting love; I have drawn you with loving-kindness. I will build you up again. (Jeremiah 31:3–4 NIV)

Of all the people on earth, the LORD *your God has chosen you to be his own special treasure.*   (Deuteronomy 7:6 NLT)

Let's pray:

Heavenly Father,

I come before You in the name of Jesus. I want to know the power of Your love. I want my life to exhibit this power in every aspect and relationship. I want to awaken strengths, not criticize the weaknesses in others. I want to use my words to build and plant lives, not tear them down. I receive Your life and love and believe I am a chosen and special treasure for You. I believe You have the power to build up my life. I give You every broken, torn-down place. Have Your way as I submit my weaknesses to You, Father. Cover them with Your strength. By the power of the Holy Spirit, reveal Your love in and through my life. Amen.

CHAPTER TEN

Two with One Heart

Earlier this year, I attended a conference where a speaker made reference to the present health of our terrestrial home. Her simple statement, "The earth is not well," impacted my life at such a deeply profound level, I found I could not shake it. Of course, a simple glance around brings this realization crashing down upon us all. But this was not what riveted me. It was the question of the why behind the earth's illness that intrigued me.

The dynamics of love, respect, protection, and honor are more than just keys to a successful marriage and intimate relationship. They are timeless principles with the ability to restore something crucial that was lost by both males and females—the power of dominion. Notice I did not say *domination*. Domination is the perversion of God's gift of strength and authority.

> *The heavens are the Lord's heavens, but the earth has He given to the children of men.* (Psalm 115:16 AMP)

Dominion is associated with ruling power, authority, or control. It describes an area of influence. It is further defined as land governed by a ruler and power over a territory. What have we done with our dominion? All authority, whether entrusted to a man or a woman, is given to serve others for their benefit and growth. The ultimate pattern for dominion was established in Genesis when God placed the man and the woman over the earth and charged them to subdue, multiply, and replenish it. Their dominion was for the well-being of the earth and its creatures. Domination benefits only the dominator at the expense of those dominated. When the man and the woman forfeited their dominion or influence, all within their domain and range of care suffered.

> *And God blessed them and told them, "Multiply and fill the earth and subdue it; you are masters of the fish and birds and all the animals. And look! I have given you the seed-bearing plants throughout the earth, and all the fruit trees for your food . . . Then God looked over all that he had made, and it was excellent in every way.*   (Genesis 1:28-31 TLB)

I love this version of the blessing. You can hear God's excitement as He empowers them. This point cannot be overemphasized: God blessed them *together* and called it "excellent in every way." Together, there was no lack or weakness. Each and every aspect was perfect.

What Men and Women Bring to the Table

The blessing is still crucial today, for it has the power to call into being whatever you might need. God gave Adam and Eve the big one. They received the earth in all its fullness. As their descendants, we have never experienced the earth and all its fullness.

Recently while in the mountains of Alaska, I was awed by a panorama of beauty. I could not imagine anything more pristine. But after thousands of years of decline, all we have ever experienced is a portion of our earth's former splendor. The first couple had it all; they possessed everything necessary to initiate order so the earth could flourish. Adam began the process when he assigned names. This established designation, position, and placement in creation. For example, the general terms "creature" and "animal" morphed into a number of specifics—horse, dog, eagle, fish, and so on—with everything named, paired, and in its place.

Then Eve came on the scene and brought her gift of relationship. She enhanced Adam's connection. Examples of this are friendship, sexual intimacy, and children. Without Eve, Adam had seed but no garden in which to plant. His seed could not produce fruit. Without the woman, the man had an abundance of food but no one to enjoy it with—no one who understood how it tasted to him. There was no one he could dream with. Without Eve, Adam was self-contained, but Eve expanded his life on every front. From the very beginning, men were about position and placement, and women were about relationship and atmosphere.

Healthy authority is for provision, protection, and direction and is rarely held entirely by one individual. It is delegated and held in common with checks and balances. Authority figures or systems are set in place to establish order so environments of every kind can flourish. If abused, authority will ultimately work against its own purpose.

For example, employers who abuse their positions will soon find employees working merely for wages rather than out of any commitment to build something that prospers. Such management may be under the mistaken impression it does not really need its workers, which fosters an attitude that employees are favored by simply being allowed to work. If leaders fail to grant their staff a sense of inclusion, the laborers are soon robbed of any sense of accomplishment. With this lack of fulfillment their enjoyment of work dies, and it becomes just a job. The passive morph into drones who simply go through the motions. The boss is frustrated by what he considers a lack of performance. He feels as though he bears the burden of the entire company as he drags them all along. Often this type of manager is unaware of his fatal mistake. By denying his employees a sense of worth, he goes it alone. They would have gladly shouldered the load if he would have shared with them a sense of value and empowerment. There is another risk pending for overbearing bosses. If there are frustrated leaders in the ranks, they will attempt to overthrow the management. Why? Because no one will work forever toward a success they will not ultimately share.

Shared Leadership

There is a similar dynamic in marriage. Man is not the boss, with the woman *doing for him*. He is the leader who *does with her*. Actually, if he is wise, he will tell her repeatedly that he can't do *without her*. I love it when my husband tells me he needs me. What is he doing? He is exercising his gift of naming and calling me "necessary." It makes me feel uniquely empowered to provide whatever he lacks. And if I don't know how to be that woman, I will do all I can to find out how. I flourish when he calls me essential.

If a man misuses his authority, you will see it reflected in his wife and children. If a woman misuses her influence, you will see it reflected in her husband. You will see embittered couples and families in conflict. In this chapter, I will focus on marriage and how God wants to restore dominion, which is the power of two with one heart.

If the husband dominates his wife, she will usually respond in one of two ways. She will cower and withdraw, or rise up against him and rebel. Sometimes this may even involve a hostile takeover. Dominating is very different from leading. Leadership includes the dignity of choice, while domination demands without options.

You will immediately recognize women who are dominated. To our shame, far too often their ranks overflow the church. After so many years of intimate mistreatment, they seem to shrink within themselves. You can actually sense their husbands' disapproval or rejection in their physical demeanor. Without a vibrant support network, these women can become shadows of the women they were before marriage.

Their confidence is usually shot, and they long ago stopped adding to their marriage relationship because everything they had was taken. They no longer volunteer ideas or opinions because they have been belittled or rejected for years. Their strength of feminine intuition is twisted into a shadowy sense of self-doubt and suspicion. They frequently disconnect and shut down sexually, because it is hard to give freely what is demanded. A woman who does not feel loved or lovely soon shrinks from any intimate touch.

She appears confused and almost incapable of making decisions. In fear, she feels the need to first run *everything* by her husband for his permission or insight. I am all for couples making decisions *together,* but I am not for the man making all the decisions for and not with his wife. Irritated, such a husband often denies his wife permission, and it is not long before she just stops asking. The woman will even shrink from her God-given authority as a mother. Often this is because the husband doesn't support the wife when she corrects or disciplines the children. Rather than experience her children's disdain, the mother remains silent. Sometimes, a woman doesn't exercise her authority because she feels overwhelmingly worthless. So hopelessly disempowered, she wonders if her children would be better off without her involvement. Her countenance is one of weary defeat. She has very few intimate friends because of the secret shame she bears. As an unloved wife, she soon withers from the touch of all. Her husband has forgotten to name her in the likeness of his love; the names "Beloved" and "Essential" are not on his lips.

The Name "Beloved" Is on *His* Lips

Do not fear, daughter, there is provision. There is Another who longs to call you by name:

> *Fear not, for I have redeemed you; I have summoned you by name; you are mine.* (Isaiah 43:1 NIV)

The Creator of heaven and earth summons you and calls you His own. And again,

"The LORD *will call you back as if you were a wife deserted and distressed in spirit—a wife who married young, only to be rejected," says your God.*   (Isaiah 54:6 NIV)

Broken ones, there is hope for you because there is One who longs not only to touch and heal your life; He will do battle on your behalf in one realm or another.

Under three things the earth trembles, under four it cannot bear up: a servant who becomes king, a fool who is full of food, an unloved woman who is married, and a maidservant who displaces her mistress.   (Proverbs 30:21–23 NIV)

Do you see this? God established the earth with such sensitivity that it trembles at the injustice of an unloved embittered woman. It quakes when a maidservant (one positioned to serve) displaces her mistress (one positioned to lead). Why would this cause the earth to shake? Is it because the health of the earth is intimately tied to both love and the healthy dominion of the man and the woman? When authority and love run amuck, the world suffers. When our God-given authority is used against allies rather than against the enemy, all of nature is caught in the resulting conflict and agony. To our

> *God established the earth with such sensitivity that it trembles at the injustice of an unloved embittered woman.*

shame, the divorce rate in the church is reported as no better than outside it. Why is it that religion is often still the most insensitive to women?

Recently, as I traveled home from Australia, I was grieved by an article I read. It seemed an Islamic Web site had published a list of parameters on how to discipline and beat a wife. It came as no surprise to me that Islam does not love its daughters. But this revelation of their intimate pain was so heartbreaking. It was a nonemotional outline of how to control a wife. The first step was to withhold sex (I guess this is their equivalent of love); if this failed, then specific beating techniques were suggested.

Is the earth even now trembling at the treatment of these daughters? Almost every country in economic turmoil is guilty of violating the rights of women. Do not imagine for a moment that these women are not precious and loved by their heavenly Father. He takes notice. Why is it the Islamic countries are among the most unstable economies and governments even though they are often richest in so many resources? They are unprofitable because they have extensive political and religious domination but not dominion. God is not callous or distant to His daughters trapped in these situations. He grieves when He sees a woman unloved.

> *When the* Lord *saw that Leah was unloved, He opened her womb.*   (Genesis 29:31 NKJV)

God often opened wombs to restore closed hearts. He gave Leah a son, to keep the love within her alive and release an arrow of legacy into her future. Domination spawns divorce, division, and loss. Dominion yields legacy. The battle between the serpent and the woman is not yet over because the complete victory has not yet been realized.

Where Is the Love?

Where is the restoration of relationships? Where is the fullness of the victory purchased by Jesus Christ, who was Eve's seed? When will we be known for our love one for another? Did Jesus come to merely give us life after death? No, He came to restore what had been lost in every relationship.

> *My purpose is to give* life in all its fullness.
>   (John 10:10 NLT, emphasis added)

And,

> *The Son of Man came to seek and to save what was lost.*
> (Luke 19:10 NIV)

This does not sound like survival until heaven; it sounds like abundance and recovery in the now. Relationships are to be full of life and the restoration of that which was lost. Too often we are so religious we hear Luke 19:10 as describing only evangelistic outreach when it carries a charge for so much more. I recently heard a leader challenge businesspeople to explore this "save what is lost" dynamic and stop feeling ashamed if God has gifted them with the ability to prosper. As I listened, my heart leaped within me. Why not extend this truth to relationships as well? Men and women can again live as one! There is the potential for restoration in every relationship that has suffered loss. Paul used the example of marriage to illustrate Christ and His church. This means we can experience this healing in our marriages now!

> *Husbands, love your wives, just as Christ loved the church and gave himself up for her . . . In this same way, husbands ought to love their wives as their own bodies. He who loves his wife loves himself.*   (Ephesians 5:25, 28 NIV)

The bottom line is: Wives are for love. How does Christ love the church? He gave up His life for us and loves us as His own. The man who loves his wife loves himself. Does this mean the man who hates his wife hates himself? I know the man who dominates his wife robs himself of all that is hers to give. By being controlling, he shuts down her fountain of life and loses her gifts of insight and tenderness. Sometimes, the woman is left with only one hope—that God will hear that she is unloved. The book of Ephesians elevates the relationship of man and woman by comparing it with Christ and the church:

> *The bottom line is:*
> *Wives are for love.*

"For this reason a man will leave his father and mother and be united to his wife, and the two will become one flesh." This is a profound mystery—but I am talking about Christ and the church. However, each one of you also must love his wife as he loves himself, and the wife must respect her husband.

(5:31–33 NIV, emphasis added)

Whom is Paul quoting when he begins, "For this reason"? He is quoting Genesis. He is reestablishing the original intent and parameters of relationship. There is more clarity given to the man's role than even to the woman's. Husbands must love, and women must respect. This definitely works, because women love to be loved, and men love to be respected.

Redemption has the power to restore all that was lost in the transgression of the Fall. The Fall not only separated us from the presence of God; we also found ourselves troubled in the company of each other. If redemption was powerful enough to restore our relationship with God, it is certainly compelling enough to reconcile us to each other. Restoration begins as we submit to the truth of God's Word and consciously choose to do it His way. Can we dare to believe husbands will again love their wives and wives will again respect their husbands? Can love and respect long gone be recovered? Yes, but not without the healing restoration of God. I have a passion to see every marriage blessed and restored to a union of passion and a legacy of dominion. Couples should join their lives because together they are stronger than each is individually.

John and I both have strengths as well as weaknesses, but when we build each other up in love, the vulnerable places become strong and the strong places become tender.

When Couples Battle

God is looking for two He can bless, but this is more than a number count; it is a heart issue and position. Often people quote the promises and know the meaning, but nothing seems to be working for them. Couples fight with each other, then wonder why it seems as though God is just not listening. Maybe you've felt this way. You know He is there and real, but there seems to be some sort of cosmic distance. You feel as though you're going through the motions, just barely surviving rather than thriving. Christianity is no longer an adventure, but a long list of do's and don'ts.

You glance around at the people in the world, and everything seems to be going great for them. Their businesses are prospering. Their marriages and sex lives seem amazing. Their lives appear to be one big party. They are guiltless and without a care as they shop incessantly and go home to their big houses. On the other hand, you wrestle with guilt as you scrimp and save.

If any of these feelings apply to you, you're not alone, but it may be time for a heart check. Let's look at an example from the book of Malachi. Things got so bad for the people of Israel that they began to accuse God of being unfair. Perhaps you have never hurled this complaint heavenward. (I know I have at least thought it really loud.) Let's look at God's response and see if we might glean some wisdom for our lives today.

> You have said, "What's the use of serving God? What have we gained by obeying his commands or by trying to show the LORD Almighty that we are sorry for our sins? From now on we will say, 'Blessed are the arrogant.' For those who do evil get rich, and those who dare God to punish them go free of harm."   (Malachi 3:14–15 NLT)

God does not sleep, but He finds constant complaining tiresome. More than likely, the people thought God was impressed with how they had couched their request as a prayer. He goes on to explain it is not that He is unjust . . . but perhaps a bit unhappy with them.

God was not their problem, and He was kind enough to tell them some reasons why things had gone awry. First, they had robbed Him through their tithes and offerings (see Malachi 3:8). They grudgingly gave Him the left over and the worst. Do you realize how serious it is to rob God? Then there was a second offense, which really upset God:

> *Here is another thing you do. You cover the LORD's altar with tears, weeping and groaning because he pays no attention to your offerings, and he doesn't accept them with pleasure. You cry out, "Why has the LORD abandoned us?" I'll tell you why! Because the LORD witnessed the vows you and your wife made to each other on your wedding day when you were young. But you have been disloyal to her, though she remained your faithful companion, the wife of your marriage vows. Didn't the LORD make you one with your wife? In body and spirit you are his. And what does he want? Godly children from your union. So guard yourself; remain loyal to the wife of your youth. "For I hate divorce!" says the LORD, the God of Israel. "It is as cruel as putting on a victim's bloodstained coat," says the LORD Almighty. "So guard yourself; always remain loyal to your wife."* (Malachi 2:13–16 NLT)

God was not honoring their prayers because they were mistreating their wives. The husbands were charged twice to guard themselves and always remain loyal to their wives. God is present when a man and a woman become one. He is there merging them, just as He was there when the one became two. God doesn't like it when someone messes with His daughters or His children. Marriage is a covenant that makes one out of two. God hates divorce because it devastates the children, and in this instance, rejected the mothers.

According to Bible scholars, during this time period the men were in such a habit of harassing their wives that when the women came before the Lord, all they could do was weep. What was meant to be a time to celebrate God's goodness became a time of mourning and distress.

How different is this from today? How many wives spend their whole prayer time crying before God because of their pain rather than celebrating their marriages? How many are like the woman who sits in services with tears streaking her face while her ex-husband sits on the other side of the building with his new, younger wife?

I thank God I go to a church that both loves and protects women. God the Father hates it when He gives us something for our good (the gift of marriage), and we turn it around for bad (the tearing apart of two who were one). Both today and in the days of Malachi, God wanted His people to come before Him with thanksgiving, filled with an overflowing love and appreciation for all He'd blessed them with. These women in the time of Malachi were so miserable, thankfulness was the last thing they could feel. They felt rejected and burdened. They were no longer loved as brides. Wives were frequently cast aside or divorced in favor of foreign and more promiscuous women.

Marriage: A Garden of Support

God always planned for our marriages to be banquets of joy and love, not some duty or obligation. God hates it when couples divorce each other emotionally as well as legally. He wants our marriages to be gardens of support and affection where both parties draw strength from each other. He wants our children raised in an atmosphere of love and laughter. I am not suggesting that anyone stay in an abusive marriage, but I am suggesting we change the way we look at marriage altogether.

I have experienced both ends of the spectrum. My parents lived as strangers in the same house. I have heard submission taught in ways that terrified young girls to even think of marrying. Who would willingly resign themselves to a life of drudgery and the loss of their individuality? I have also seen men railroaded and belittled by their wives.

> *Marriage should never mean loss to either party.*

Marriage should never mean loss to either party. God created a hunger in Adam for companionship, and then He formed Eve to fulfill this need. It was God, not the man, who originally determined it was not good for the man to be alone, and it was God who blessed what they did together.

There is the capacity for increase whenever the two are one. Increase is not limited to just having children; it encompasses everything. What might happen if we began to walk as one? Everyone would win.

There was a season of intense struggle and disagreement in our marriage. John and I were at an impasse, and rather than continuing to fight openly, we slipped into a cold war. We were measured lovers and friends who came only so close, but no closer. John was busy traveling, and I was busy with children. Our orbits spun independently. It just seemed easier that way. I did not bother him, and he did not bother me. Separate lives seemed safer. I felt if I showed him that I really needed him, I would be giving him yet another opportunity to hurt and disappoint me. Sadly, I believe John felt the same way. We were willing to reach out and touch others, but not each other. There was a disconnect. It was as though we'd experienced an amicable divorce, without formal papers. One morning I woke early and was writing in my journal when the Holy Spirit quickened my heart with the following Scripture:

Do two walk together unless they have agreed to do so?

(Amos 3:3 NIV)

We were walking but there was no agreement. We only agreed to disagree and, frankly, for a husband and a wife that is just not good enough. I felt the prompting continue: *What I want to do will not happen with the two of you functioning separately . . . I want two who are one, for this is what I can bless.*

Later, I shared with John what I felt God had told me. I told him I was with and for him, and that I had no interest in living life without him. John softened and shared his desire to do the same. We joined hands and hearts that day. We laid it all down—the distance, the opinions, the who was right, and the who was wrong. We gave it all to the

Father in prayer: "Holy Father, bless us again . . . make us one." It was both a definite and dramatic turning point in our relationship, family, finances, and ministry.

When a Wife Abuses Her Power

Two are better than one, because they have a good return for their work. (Ecclesiastes 4:9 NIV)

Each marriage partner was meant to bring increase and blessing into the life of the other. Domination happens when authority and strength are misused or abused by the husband. But what happens when the wife misuses her power?

The woman has the ability to influence and create an environment that fosters intimate relationship in the marriage. When influence goes bad, it mutates into something rather frightening called manipulation. Manipulation is often the chosen tack, because a wife may be afraid that if she is not in control, she will be hurt. She is motivated by self-protection rather than by love.

Most daughters today are not schooled in wisdom and influence. All they have known is manipulation and the art of seduction. To manipulate something means to exploit its weakness for your advantage. In the case of the husband, this weakness is often his heart or his ability to communicate it effectively. If the dynamic is healthy, a woman should actually be sensitive to the male ego, rather than toy with his weakness.

Manipulation can take many forms. A wife can withhold respect from her husband and make him feel vulnerable and naked. A woman can flatter her husband in order to get what she wants. Both processes prey upon his weakness. He has a valid need to be admired and respected. Usually someone who extends empty flattery is bribing the other person.

This is altogether different from sincerely complimenting your husband. All wives should regularly and sincerely compliment their husbands to build them up. This creates an atmosphere of safety for the men (and the children). Likewise, smart husbands will compliment their wives to surround them with their love. The wives will blossom with affection and attraction.

Here's a case in point: Samson had a weakness for women. He was exhausted and just looking for a place to rest his head, when Delilah exploited his weakness for her own advantage. When intimacy goes wrong, it twists into seduction, and the man's need for the woman is used against him rather than for him. In this dynamic, the man's strength is decreased rather than multiplied. But it is not just the men who have dealt treacherously with the partners of their youth.

> *To deliver you from the immoral woman, from the seductress who flatters with her words, who forsakes the companion of her youth, and forgets the covenant of her God. For her house leads down to death, and her paths to the dead; none who go to her return, nor do they regain the paths of life.*
> (Proverbs 2:16–19 NKJV)

The seductress uses her words to flatter and deceive, rather than to bless and build. She abandons her husband and breaks covenant with God. As if this were not enough, she also leads others astray. Her victims confuse her paths of pleasure and promiscuity for life, when really they are entrances to the realm of death. Wisdom openly calls to all, but seduction whispers secretively.

> *With her enticing speech she caused him to yield, with her flattering lips she seduced him.* (Proverbs 7:21 NKJV)

Enticing speech and flattering words are the tools of seduction. Notice that he is taken captive by her words. Words have the power to capture or release, to build or to destroy. The seductress steals life, while the wise woman preserves it. Because wisdom is a tree of life.

Be an Expert on Your Husband's Strengths

I cannot even begin to tell you of all the broken and depleted areas of life I brought into my marriage. John had issues of his own as well, but discussion never worked when all we did was point out the vulnerabilities of each other. No one has the potential to be as close as a husband and a wife. God never intended intimate friends to be experts at each other's weaknesses.

I know where I am weak. John knows where he is weak. We are in each other's lives to help make the weak strong. Where is the strength in highlighting or focusing on our spouses' weaknesses? As discussed earlier, all are better served by speaking to strengths. If a city's protection was in the strong wall that encompassed it, how would this defense be enhanced by pointing out flaws or breaches? The broken places would be the very locations we should strengthen and fortify. We repair so the weak may be strong rather than repeatedly call them weak.

Somewhere along the way, John and I discovered leveling criticism just was not working, so rather than pointing out each other's deficiencies, we began to rebuild our lives by elaborating on each other's strengths. This meant focusing on the good and the admirable. This also included some widespread change on multiple levels.

First, I changed the way I spoke to John. Next, I changed what I said about him to others. Third, I made a conscious choice not to hang out with women who slammed men. This is really common sense, for I would hope my husband would not socialize with men who dishonored women. No matter how impervious you might imagine you are, disparaging comments will eventually affect your perspective. Male bashing is not cool, even if you don't add to others' comments. Know that such comments will deter you in your pursuit of truth and honor.

I also choose to not spend time with women who openly discuss their sex lives with others. I am not talking about those who are advising others or those seeking help or counsel, but rather those who would tell me private, intimate details about their husbands. These were things I did not want to hear, and the next time I saw their husbands, I was a bit embarrassed that I had heard their tales.

What happens in both marriage and the marriage bed is to be a source of strength, life, and sustenance. Repeatedly the book of Proverbs likens the intimate life in marriage to a joyous fountain of life. How can these waters remain sweet if they are shared by so many others? Talking about intimate experiences as though they were a conquest or something out of *Cosmopolitan* magazine is not godly. The book of James comments on the power of our speech:

> *Can both fresh water and salt water flow from the same spring? My brothers, can a fig tree bear olives, or a grapevine bear figs? Neither can a salt spring produce fresh water.*
>
> (3:11–12 NIV)

We will always release what is in us. If it is fresh and life-giving, it will be refreshing, but if it looks like water but cannot bring life, beware. You cannot drink salt water, and it stings the eyes and dries the skin. It is fun to swim in, but offers no real respite to the thirsty. Only God can make us flow in His living water.

> *Drink water from your own cistern, running water from your own well. Should your springs overflow in the streets, your streams of water in the public squares? Let them be yours alone, never to be shared with strangers. May your fountain be blessed, and may you rejoice in the wife of your youth. A loving doe, a graceful deer—may her breasts satisfy you always, may you ever be captivated by her love.*
>
> (Proverbs 5:15–19 NIV)

I love this poetic and intimate description of love in marriage. In our homes it runs clean and pure. The woman should have the power to captivate her husband with her love. When marriage overflows into the streets by way of adultery, pornography, or impure conversation, it becomes muddied and the portion of strangers. What is beautiful between two becomes dirty among many. When we share our intimate lives with others, we destroy the portion that is sacred.

Weathering the Storms

We are not just to be merely in bed, we are to be together for both warmth and protection.

> *Also, if two lie down together, they will keep warm. But how can one keep warm alone? Though one may be overpowered, two can defend themselves.*　　　(Ecclesiastes 4:11–12 NIV)

We are not promised a storm-free life, but we can determine how well we weather it. Through more than two decades of trial and error, I have found the following truth to repeatedly ring true: The inclement weather and storms outside my marriage are no real threat, as long as inside my marriage there is a place of safety and warmth. The storms within marriage have the power to threaten and overwhelm us. No matter what rages against us in the course of the day, at the end of it, we must determine to lie down with each other in warmth.

I am sure you know you can sleep in the same bed yet experience no affection. When two stretch the limits of their king-sized bed in an effort to withhold comfort from each other, both will lose. I don't know where your marriage has been. I don't know what storm rages right outside your bedroom window. You can't control what is on the outside, but you can choose not to let it in. If you have allowed outside pressure to exert itself within, you can change that tonight.

Our husbands should be respected as our most intimate of friends. Wives should be adored and entrusted with the issues of their husbands' hearts. Couples should be more in love as their marriages progress than they were in the beginning. They should enjoy the blessing of shared history and legacy.

A cord of three strands is not quickly broken.

(Ecclesiastes 4:12 NIV)

I believe an example of this triple-strength cord can be found in the entwining of the respected husband with the loved wife and the seeds or heirs of their union. Because of the ravages of divorce, many of us did not inherit a legacy of sound finance, love, or life, but today that can change. The reestablishment of and potential for legacy are available again with each generation. Let's fight as one.

———————

Heavenly Father,

I come to you in the name of Jesus. Re-create in our marriage the dynamic of two who have one heart. Bless us again with the power of dominion, and forgive us for using our strengths against each other. I choose to respect my husband in word and deed. I want our lives to weave a legacy for our children. Awaken our love again. Restore the warmth, strength, and intimacy with my husband. Surround me with godly friends who encourage growth in my marriage. Give me the discernment to know the changes and adjustments I need to make to see this happen. Forgive me for misusing my words and influence in any way, shape, or form. Forgive me for complaining against You. Father, You are more than generous and good. I commit to create an atmosphere in my home that You can bless. I choose to walk as one and recover our power of dominion. Amen.

———————

CHAPTER ELEVEN

Fighting for Beauty

Even in the midst of almost universal upheaval there are some constants. The longing for youth and beauty remains. Everywhere you look, you see its desperate cry as this ceaseless quest continues. We must ask, *Why* all this emphasis on ageless beauty? I believe our answer is found in beauty's connection with our deeper human longing . . . a desperate cry for love. It is difficult to pick up a magazine, watch a television show, or visit a store without being confronted by this hunger.

Not only do we want to be beautiful . . . we want beauty to surround us. We want to experience it in all we see, touch, taste, and smell. Thus the transformation or makeover of homes, bodies, wardrobes, gardens, rooms, and in some cases even towns has begun. But is this drive and desire toward the makeover wrong? Perhaps the approach is somewhat misguided, but not the desire. For it is God who originated this all-encompassing pursuit of beauty as well as our desire to see it realized.

He has made everything beautiful in its time.

(Ecclesiastes 3:11 NIV)

Notice this verse does not say He *will* make everything beautiful in its time, but it declares *He has made everything* beautiful. All things, not just some things; and *every* one, not just some, are seeded with beauty. We carry both the promise and the hope of beauty within us. We are predestined for splendor and loveliness. There no longer remains a question of whether ageless beauty can happen . . . it will. The question becomes a matter of when and where.

> **We are predestined for splendor and loveliness.**

In another time and place, beauty will no longer be free to discriminate and grace some and not others. There, beauty will be given to all. This gives rise to another question: If beauty is for all, when will it be our turn? How long before everyone and everything is robed again in splendor?

In addition to the quest for beauty, God created within us an abiding hope that the old would somehow be made new. Notice I did not say for the old to become *young,* but for the old to become *new.* To be young again is not enough. There are those who may initially argue this point with me. Weary and worn by the years they've traveled, they may wag tired heads and murmur, "I'm exhausted. I've lived long enough; I don't want to have to do it all over again." Please understand, I am not speaking of rewinding life so you can start again, nor am I suggesting the recapturing of youth with the added benefit of knowledge and lessons this life has taught. Neither approach captures the essence or breadth of what I speak of. We watch for something so much more than a chronological displacement or mask of youth over the wisdom of age. No, our destiny is pregnant with something no *mortal* eyes have seen; something, therefore, we can scarcely hope to believe exists. We can be confident in this, for we are told,

*No eye has seen, no ear has heard, no mind has conceived
what God has prepared for those who love him.*

                                        (1 Corinthians 2:9 NIV)

We watch for what we have not seen. We listen for sounds unfamiliar to us, and stretch beyond ourselves to embrace dreams and ideas our minds cannot even receive in seed form. The awesome magnitude of this promise defies the boundaries of our imaginations. Long ago, God planted these longings in the soil of human hearts, knowing someday they would call us back to Him.

For All Who Love Him

Though mortal, we long for the immortal and eternal. There resides within us an inborn desire for something so extremely outside our realm and reach, it cannot help but awe us. This could never be something we'd ever hope to attain. I pause in wonder at the beauty and simplicity of what qualifies us for such unimaginable ecstasy. He prepares this for *those who love Him.*

I might be frightened and fear disqualification if these preparations were for those He loves. But we have no need to fear. It is an all-encompassing banquet of amazement for those who love Him. I don't even believe we have the capacity to verbalize our love for Him. When I feel I can't express my love enough toward one of my boys, I will just say, "I love you more than more." But quite honestly, as much as I truly love them, I am completely imperfect in the expression of my motherly love. Perhaps as I hold them in my embrace, they catch a fleeting glimpse of the perfect love of Another.

Our hunger exceeds our capacity to imagine. God often reveals imperfection to create a desire for His perfection. Though we've neither seen nor heard, there is a revelation for those who hunger for more.

But God has revealed it to us by his Spirit.

                                        (1 Corinthians 2:10 NIV)

There is a place that has the capacity to grasp this revelation . . . the heart. It is where the Spirit whispers and woos (speaking glorious mysteries) to us as the veil of heaven and earth thins with the passage of time.

We watch and wait for a metamorphic renewal so profound it is capable of breaking us free from every limitation and the bands of humanity. We are destined for an encounter so powerful it will wrench us from the very bonds of time itself. This is the type of makeover that awaits each and every child of God.

Why Is Eternity Planted in Our Hearts?

Our present cry for beauty and restoration is merely a glimpse. I believe we'll experience an utterly complete transformation on every level. I've seen this cry even at the close of life when all hope of youth is lost. I saw its reflection when I kissed my grandmother good-bye for the last time. She was a bent shadow of the beauty she had once been. A wispy halo of white hair adorned her head. The hand I held was sheathed in skin so spotted and paper-thin I had to strain to remember the tanned socialite of years gone by. To comfort myself, I imagined her skin was thinning in preparation for her departure. She would soon step free of a garment that was too thin and old to hold her any longer. She had fallen, and I no longer recognized her smile because her teeth were broken and discolored. My younger children had never met her before. They hung back a bit, frightened as I kissed her forehead and tucked her in that last time. As I leaned close, I realized all the fragrance that had surrounded her in my youth had fled. I knew I would not see her again until the old are made new.

> *He has made everything beautiful in its time. He has also set eternity in the hearts of men.* (Ecclesiastes 3:11–12 NIV)

Why would God set eternity in the hearts of His mortal children? Was it to frustrate us? No, I believe it was to cause us to lift our eyes beyond the realm of the seen, heard, and thought. Eternity in the hearts of men causes us to live beyond this moment and live for a time and place yet unseen.

Death is an uncomfortable fit for the sons and daughters of Adam and Eve. We do not wear its corruption well, for it is in fact our enemy. Could this be why we not only want the ugly duckling to grow into a beautiful swan, but we also want to see the old, tired swan somehow retain its place of dignity and honor throughout its life? As sons and daughters of Adam and Eve, it is only right that we would fight death and destruction and the theft of beauty on every front. To this end, we long to see weakness and frailty turned into strength, diseases cured, and destruction and poverty overturned. Likewise, we wrestle with issues of purpose and authority because our garden has been overrun and our dominion compromised. At some level, we all hope to dig deep enough to find our buried treasure unearthed . . . and we will.

We long to see cluttered lives and rooms organized and their occupants empowered. I recently marveled as one lucky woman's room was transformed from utter chaos to a haven of creativity. As she stood surveying the handiwork of the designers, she even looked different. She looked somewhat straighter, less cluttered and earthbound. She wore the room well because now she could reach out and lay hold of her tools, dreams, and possessions. She could enjoy what she'd always had but was unable to extract from all her mess. It had always been there for her; she just needed it rearranged and grouped logically. When another with a different perspective came alongside her, together they walked through what had become too overwhelming for her to face alone.

We all have access to this wise Other.

> *And I will ask the Father, and he will give you another Counselor to be with you forever.*   (John 14:16 NIV)

The Holy Spirit's counsel is more than a twenty-four-hour intensive with cameras and TV personalities, where sooner or later the forward progression halts and participants spiral back down to the routine of the day-to-day. I don't want to be negative, but no matter how extensive the transformation of a room, the occupant must be trained or transformed in order for the makeover to be maintained.

How many Christians are the same as some of these makeover contestants? In a moment or a meeting, they experience radical, life-changing transformation, only to slip back into their old patterns and ways as soon as the action abates. Their makeover from death to life becomes nothing more than a memory. The transformation of the moment no longer exerts itself on their present. This is exactly the opposite of what is supposed to be.

Lasting Transformation

The path of the righteous is like the first gleam of dawn, shining ever brighter till the full light of day. (Proverbs 4:18 NIV)

This verse has always been one of my favorites. It lends poetic perspective to my journey. For us, the moment of change should not be our highlight but merely the beginning. It should be the point in time when our light is the dimmest, yielding the very faintest outline of the road before us. Not unlike the Wizard of Oz's fictional yellow-brick road, we should find our way increasingly illuminated as we near our destination.

I'll never forget my son's reaction to a visit we made to the desolate trailer home of an AIDS victim. She was a young single mother who'd been kicked out of her parents' home and was living with the abusive boyfriend who had fathered her child and transmitted the virus. I brought my son with me when I delivered a small dresser, some clothes, and food for her and the baby. At the time, my son was no more than eight, and he literally cowered as he looked around at the filth and disorder of the small trailer. I had hoped to train him by way of example in outreach, but instead I watched as he shrank within himself, obviously repulsed.

As we drove home, I asked him why he had reacted that way. He answered me truthfully, "Mommy, it scared me." I thought a moment and, in truth, I as well had been frightened by the hopelessness of the scene. Death and neglect shadowed the life of an infant, while a young and selfish couple spiraled toward further destruction. Everything in their dwelling spelled despair, from the clothes tossed on the floor to the uncashed government check and unredeemed food vouchers on the table. They were careless with what they had, and therefore poorer than any could imagine. Often the greatest poverty comes when we fail to realize what we have, just as the greatest deception comes when we do not know who we are.

> *He has made everything beautiful in its time. He has also set eternity in the hearts of men; yet they cannot fathom what God has done from beginning to end.* (Ecclesiastes 3:11 NIV)

Longing for Redemption

God put this longing and hope for redemption in each of us, but it is frightening when we lose sight of it. Without it, we have no true perspective. From eternal vantages, we should welcome the desire to see order come out of our disorder. Youth springs forth from old age as the old puts on the new.

This is the very reason why visual before-and-after images hold such a desperate fascination for some of us. At some level or another, we love the whole concept of the makeover, and you know what? We were meant to.

I have to wonder if this intrigue was knit into the fiber of each and every one at the time of creation. We see this dynamic come into play even at the moment of birth. As sons and daughters of Adam and Eve, our first breath begins our journey toward death. I know even saying this seems somehow wrong; even though we know it to be true, it is an uncomfortable fit for most of us. As children of light, we will never wear death and decay well, for the truth is, none of us were ever formed for it. Of all created beings, we (men and women) alone were created in the image of God, the Giver of life. It would stand to reason, then, that death and every other theft of our vitality goes against the very nature of the image in which we were created. This is one reason we should always fight to preserve life.

We alone, God's pinnacle of creation, grapple with the shadowy fear of death and wage war against the wrinkling curse of aging. Could this struggle emanate from us because we've lost our covering? Furless, we alone so obviously wear the signs of our aging and the passage of time like a road map of our lives.

Removing the Terror of Death

Animals do not fear death; they fight it. Their drive to survive is different from our own. Animals do not strive against the embrace of death or complain of the destruction time wreaks upon their bodies.

For them, death is not an enemy to fear; it is only another enemy to fight in an attempt to survive. Survival is their goal because all they live for is found on earth, but survival alone should never be enough for us. We want something more. We want victory over death, for death is our final foe.

> *The last enemy to be destroyed is death.*
>
> (1 Corinthians 15:26 NIV)

And,

> *Then the saying that is written will come true: "Death has been swallowed up in victory."* (1 Corinthians 15:54 NIV)

God our Father understood this terror that the shadow of death would hold for each of us, so He confronted this fear, and by the power of the cross changed its name . . . and there is such incredible power in a name. Jesus changed the name of *death,* which means "loss," to *sleep,* which means "rest." For His beloved children, death no longer represents finality or an end; it becomes the beginning of a dream. We find an example of this when Jesus addressed the wailing mourners in Matthew 9:24: "'Go away. The girl is not dead but asleep.' But they laughed at him" (NIV). He was even then foreshadowing the promise to come. The Word of God tells us:

> Listen, I tell you a mystery: We will not all sleep, but we will
> all be changed.   (1 Corinthians 15:51 NIV)

Don't we all sleep most every day? Then obviously Paul was not referring to nightly or daily rest. He had adopted the language of the Spirit, and in his writings he began to call death "sleep." We are told we will not all sleep (rest), but we will all change. The word *change* can mean "to alter, transform, or revolutionize." The Greek word for "to change" means "to be changed" in many applications. There are two paths into this type of change: sleeping or being captured at His reappearing.

For reasons known only to our Father, rest is often the precursor to deep change. Some of us will never experience the sleep of death, yet all who are God's own are promised this change. Jesus experienced the full-force agony of death so we would not have to experience its terror. For His children, there is only sleep and then a change; and for some just the change awaits them.

We'll See True Beauty

And such a change this world has never seen. It will be a "before and after" so extensive that no photo or hour-long program could ever hope to capture its many facets or extent. I believe we will look at ourselves and actually see true beauty for the first time. We will look at one another and gasp in wonder at the loveliness and the power of it all. Like children, I imagine we will hug and cry and squeal, "Is it you? . . . Because it's really me!"

It is the very thing we glimpse here in shadow form. Shadows are not wrong; the problem is they have no lasting substance and flee before the brilliance of light. Instead of sitting back and making commentary on the virtue or vice of the whole makeover dynamic, extreme or otherwise, it is time to acknowledge that there is a change coming for which we all long. The world knows it in this world of shadow, but do we truly know it in the realm of substance? As God's daughters, we steward an awesome truth. It is time to allow it to transform us.

> *When the perishable has been clothed with the imperishable,*
> *and the mortal with immortality, then the saying that is writ-*
> *ten will come true: "Death has been swallowed up in victory."*
> (1 Corinthians 15:54 NIV)

As I pondered this, I found the parallels extensive. Think of it. Those who undergo plastic surgery or an extreme makeover of any kind are first consulted about their desires and expectations. Then the realism of these expectations is discussed. The surgeon may say, "We can do this, but it will look like this rather than that. I can't give you Ashley Judd's exact cheeks, but this is how close I can get." (Her beautiful smile has made her cheeks the most requested.) Then, with most procedures, implants and/or incisions are discussed in detail. Then there is the amount of time necessary for the healing process and the risks involved with the procedure. And finally, the amount of money it will cost to achieve these results is tallied. And then the patient must weigh the promise, the pain, the recovery, and the price.

They are put to sleep whole, and though they realize they will wake up swollen and in pain, and more often than not with some marks and scars, there remains the promise of a difference. Something will be changed or rearranged, and though they may suffer pain, if they will endure the healing and wait patiently for the swelling to subside, they will discover beauty on the other side of the process.

God's promise to us is sort of a flipped version of this. In His makeover we go to sleep wounded and scarred, aged and worn, perhaps even sagging and swollen, and we wake up pain-free, new, youthful, fresh, and strong.

I have been sedated twice. Anesthesia is a form of suspended life. It is an excessively deep sleep state where the patient loses all contact with both pain and reality as they knew it. The body is experiencing all sorts of things, but the mind does not perceive it. The first time I was placed under anesthesia was when they removed my eye at age five. I went to sleep with two eyes and woke up with one. More recently I went under anesthesia to reset my nose, which I'd broken surfing. There was a major breathing and ear-clearing issue due to my injury. I was forty-three at the time, but because of my former surgery when I was five, I found myself terrified at the prospect of going under anesthesia again. Talk about the ultimate loss of control! I remember as I scheduled the surgery with the receptionist, I began to shake involuntarily.

I had a wonderful, caring doctor, and I knew I needed to do this, but the fear remained. I made John stay with me until they wheeled me into the operating room. My doctor spoke softly to me as I went under and was there to encourage me when I awoke. The last thing I remembered was being asked a question: "So how did you really break your nose . . . did your husband punch you?"

Before I could even answer, I was gone. I woke up answering the question, "No! I broke it . . . !"

I realized there had been a skip in time. My answer changed to a question in mid-sentence: ". . . did you already do it?"

"Yes, and you did fabulous!" the kind doctor answered.

I was so relieved it was over, I was giddy.

John came into the recovery room and I repeated what the doctor said: "Honey, I did fabulous!"

This time I had not suffered loss; I had been repaired. All the way home I was beside myself with elation. The process was over. I had not had something removed, but a nose reconnected and made whole.

I believe this is a shadow of the type of process that awaits each of us if we will allow the Holy Spirit to have His way. We will go under afraid, but awaken to find that a process was completed while we rested in Him.

> *Therefore we do not lose heart. Though outwardly we are wasting away, yet inwardly we are being renewed day by day.* (2 Corinthians 4:16 NIV)

What God Sees

Can you believe God can make you over and flip you inside out? I believe Christian women can be lovely all through their lives. We need to show this to the world. Along with our desire for beauty, there has been a bit of a twist. It appears the uniqueness of the individual is under aggressive attack. Let's look at this from the flip side. Something is definitely amiss. I believe the enemy of our souls is slightly afraid that we will wake up and become who we truly are.

Why else would women (both the young and the old) be so incessantly harassed to empty themselves of all that is valuable and focus solely on the external? Why would women leave behind the strengths of wisdom and the heritage of legacy to embrace foolishness and fleeting momentary pleasure? In this whirlwind of the unreal and undone, what should a Christian woman look like? How should she act? How should she dress? What should her voice sound like? These are questions I want to help you answer. Because within you lies a piece, a part, a role, a voice, a design, and even a look that we all need.

Recently I was at a conference where the Spirit brought forth this word, which expresses how He views us:

> *When I look at you I see something more . . . I see promise.*
> *I see a generation of daughters so terrifying to the enemy*

that he will do whatever he can in his power to distort your image, pervert your beauty, and rob you of your strength and power.

He is the father of lies and speaks to you through a glass but darkly. But the Father of Light longs to speak to you face-to-face.

He wants to touch the dark places where the wounding is so deep and severe it threatens to define your very existence.

> He will reach beyond the glass and call you altogether lovely and His own.

Ask, and He will allow you to behold Him. He will reach beyond the glass and call you all-together lovely and His own.

The king is enthralled by your beauty; honor him, for he is your lord.   (Psalm 45:11 NIV)

How do we honor our Lord when it comes to the issue of our beauty? We accept His words as the ultimate truth. He called your beauty enthralling; do you dare call Him a liar? Will you be brave enough to receive His love? Let this vantage embrace you. Actually, you cannot trust the mirror; you are so much more than what you see! Let's pray,

Heavenly Father,
I come before You in the name of the One who is altogether lovely, Jesus the Christ. You are making me over from the inside out. I want the countenance of a woman who refuses to give way to fear. Forgive me for saying things contrary to Your Word, which is alive. Father, You are the Great Physician and the One capable of perfecting every area of my life.

We women can be lovely before You and others no matter our age.

I repent of looking to the graven image and idols of this world when I should have come to You for my strength. I renounce their hold and influence. I cast their impressions from my mind and their illusions from before my eyes. Lord, remove their veil from my eyes; I want to see You and You alone. Let Your image outshine any other in my life. Imprint me deeper than any other. Reveal Yourself to me in an intimate and real way. I give You permission to invade this private and personal area of my life. Amen.

CHAPTER TWELVE

Flawed but Authentic

As I travel, I hear a lot of talk about the importance of *being real*. As time has passed, I have learned to question whether "real" is, well, really enough. We all know being fake will just not get us where we need to go. Though heaven knows, enough of us have tried to navigate life via the unreal. I find myself with a persistent hunger for something more. There remains a longing for a dynamic that encompasses the realm of something deeper and more enduring.

For years I've heard one form or another of these comments after speaking at conferences:

- "I love it that you are so free . . . so real."
- "Thanks for being real."
- "I love it that you're so transparent."

Free is good, and transparent is important, but the *real* has always tripped me up a bit. Now, mind you, I realize all these phrases are meant to be complimentary. But sometimes I find myself wishing for something more. Like, "Wow, you are so profound," or "You're really deep." Maybe even an occasional "Your presentation was so intellectually sound and professional" would be nice. Instead, I get the hug and the recurring comment: "Sister, thanks for keeping it real."

Of course, I don't want the unflattering alternative to *real*. Who in their right mind would want to be labeled a fake or a fraud? I definitely don't want to be called a fraud; it's just that I was hoping to be labeled something a bit more unusual, unique, or difficult to attain. While flying home from a speaking engagement I was again reflecting on this whole ideal of "real," and I sensed the Spirit speaking to me.

> *Lisa, I am looking for something more. You can be a real piece of wood, and when you go into the fire you'll come out a real pile of ashes. I am looking for more than "real" in you; I want to work with the authentic.*

I realized from this that something can be real without being authentic. A copy of a Monet is real, but it is not an authentic Monet. This was a visual if I'd ever had one, and I knew what it meant: I was going back into a fire of some sort. Maybe "real" was more of a comfortable fit for me than I'd first realized.

It has been my Christian life experience that the term *fire* usually translates into a test or, in my case, tests. I almost always end up taking the more difficult retest because I just didn't get it the first time around. I also suspected testing would be involved because you usually don't have to test something to discover if it is real or not; normally you can tell just by touching it or, in some cases, the smell will clue you in.

For example, *is that flower arrangement real?* You have to know, so you slip in close and inhale or gently touch it . . . No, it's a fake. *Is that real glass?* You pick it up; it's lightweight and sounds a bit hollow when you thump it. No, it's plastic. *Is that fur over there real?* I am always compelled to pet it, and of course then I know.

I have to be honest, I am tired of silk flowers with their plastic, dusty fragrance. The fake petals tend to absorb the odors of what surrounds them rather than emanate a fragrance from within. For a long time I have wanted to smell the beauty of the Lord and feel His presence. It is where I find myself truly alive!

I have grown a bit tired of controlled beauty. I know living flowers cost more to maintain, but I prefer experiencing a single rose over an entire bouquet of silk and plastic. I want the blossom to let me know if it's feeling a bit wilted. I want to drop the fragile petals into the pages of my Bible and hang the flowers upside down to dry in my closet. Better yet, give me something alive and growing, and let me be part of making it blossom and bloom.

Are you with me on this one? Are you looking for something more than the silk-flower version of your present Christian reality? Have we settled for the unreal because we're afraid to hope for something more? Do we think it might be too much to ask for the authentic? Where is the authentic change? Where is the genuine character? Where is the power?

Seeing Through the Fruit to the Tree

Years ago, I invited God to continually weave His divine dissatisfaction into the fabric of my life. I gave Him permission one day to excavate my life, to dig deep and go after some of the root issues. I was tired of continually plucking the visible fruit of deeper issues while pretending the tree did not exist. Before this encounter with truth, I had prayed prayers that invited God to only landscape and accessorize my life. They went something like this: "Father, surround my life with pretty and pleasant things. Accessorize my life with beauty because You love me."

But in a moment that all changed. I wanted to move beyond being loved by Him. I wanted to love Him with my whole heart and worship Him in

> *I wanted to cry over His beauty rather than look at His goodness.*

spirit and truth. I wanted to cry over His beauty rather than look at His goodness. I knew I needed to lift my eyes from the earthbound and allow Him to delve into the soil of my heart. The pure in heart will see Him. I wanted to see and experience Him on a more intimate genuine level. I was no longer content to simply repeat His promises; I needed to hear His heart. With this prayer the working of the authentic began and continues yet today.

Authentic items are usually tested at a level deeper than superficial touch. For instance, how you felt when you hugged or smelled something doesn't really count when you are looking for an authentic item. It runs a bit deeper. I remember hearing how one of my college classmates claimed academic skills he did not have and landed himself a great job. He just put the false information down on his résumé, and no one checked to see if it was authentic. In areas of our own lives as well, at times something can look authentic and sound authentic, but when we check the references, we realize the truth.

I guess some of us who have been slated as real need to be careful we are not just real *carnal*. I have heard fleshly behavior excused by saying, "Hey, I'm just being real!" Not only is fleshly behavior unattractive, it does not accurately represent our value or the price that was paid to authenticate us as genuinely His.

I sometimes think there is too short a connection between my brain and my mouth. I will say something without thinking only to regret it later. If it's only about keeping it real, then why did God warn us repeatedly to be careful with our words? If we are not authentic, our thoughtless reactions and words may confuse others.

> *[Sisters,] you have no obligation whatsoever to do what your sinful nature urges you to do. For if you keep on following it, you will perish. But if through the power of the Holy Spirit you turn from it and its evil deeds, you will live. For all who are led by the Spirit of God are children of God.*
>
> (Romans 8:12–14 NLT)

The ability to live over and above our immediate emotional dictates and reactions (regardless of hormonal fluctuations) is a God-given, Spirit-breathed gift of grace. When we are no longer motivated by the earthly human need for acceptance, we will not feel driven to repeatedly prove ourselves right. We can rise above this and be empowered to turn from the very entanglements that trap others. Christian relational dynamics should be revolutionary in a world steeped in offense, slander, and revenge. We should look different.

The Power to Bless When Cursed

Bless those who curse you, pray for those who mistreat you. If someone strikes you on one cheek, turn to him the other also. If someone takes your cloak, do not stop him from taking your tunic.

(Luke 6:28–29 NIV)

Who in their right mind wants to bless those who curse them? Who physically enjoys being slapped even once, let alone offering their cheek a second time? Your immediate "real" reaction is, "All right, I've had it, and I am going to curse you and slap you back harder than you slapped me!" Only authentic children, those led by God's Holy Spirit, can bless and turn away when they really want to curse and hit. This is often not your initial reaction, but it should be your follow-through.

When someone repeatedly speaks against you, there is a choice. You can try to do your own damage control, or you can get God involved. The dynamic may be different with you, but I have learned I just don't do damage control well. I am always under the mistaken impression that if I can figure it out, then I can fix it. The truth is, there is just so much you can do, and then you have to surrender it to the Father. There is just so much you can say, and then you have said too much.

There have been times when I have sent two-sentence notes of blessing. Each time I heard a derogatory report I sent a blessing the other way. Why? Is that really what I felt like doing? No way . . . those were not my real feelings, but it was an authentic response, which invites the love of God into the lives of both people. Do I authentically love the person even if I don't like what they're doing? I must, for that is the only way to keep my spirit clear. If we submit to the statutes of God's Word to love, then He is involved in what happens. After that, it is up to Him.

> *Love your enemies! Pray for those who persecute you! In that way, you will be acting as true [authentic] children of your Father in heaven. For he gives his sunlight to both the evil and the good, and he sends rain on the just and on the unjust, too.*
> (Matthew 5:44–45 NLT)

We are proved to be authentic children by our reactions and responses to our enemies. It is often painfully true that we have perceived enemies in the body of Christ. I say *perceived* because can any part of one's body truly be an enemy to the rest? Sadly, often we Christians are still working on being nice to one another and our loved ones.

Our response to our enemies, whether perceived or actual, is how we emulate or model our Father's behavior in this world. God is truth, and therefore He is our ultimate example of what it means to be authentic. This means He is consistent in His character of goodness to both the righteous and the unrighteous. He does not vary toward us because of our variance or faithlessness toward Him. This brings us to another point: authentic items are consistent. An item cannot be authentic one moment and fake the next.

Therefore, authentic individuals are the same no matter where they are. Their atmosphere or environment does not control them or dictate their godliness or the lack thereof. They are the same in their business dealings as they are in their church. They are the same in private as they are in public. Those who are authentic live truthfully and authentically, and this distinguishes them as being over and above the surface level of real. Remember the example of wood to which I referred at the beginning of this chapter? Wood definitely is not the same in the fire as it is out of it! Authentic items and individuals come out of the fire stronger. Real items come out of the fire having suffered loss.

Treating Things—and People—According to Their Value

The terms *authentic* and *genuine* are often used when referring to crystal, jewels, stones, gold, silver, or other precious metals. You rarely hear someone say, "This goblet is authentic glass." *Authentic* could be used when referring to crystal, which is more refined and processed than glass and therefore more costly. From what I understand, crystal starts out purer and stays in the heat a bit longer than regular glass.

Of course, there are times in this life when neither crystal nor glass will do. Because I have four sons, we have broken a countless number of *real* glasses. I purchased twenty-four *plastic* glasses because they could be bounced on the floor and still looked like glass until you actually handled them. Neither glass nor crystal bounces, so both should be carefully handled.

As a general rule, the more refined the object, the more care or honor in its treatment. Crystal goblets are even washed differently from glass ones. You can run both glass and plastic through the dishwasher, but you better not do this with the crystal. You can damage its luster or even break it. The more extensive refining process does not mean it will necessarily be more durable. This analogy immediately brings to my remembrance the way God described the careful and tender handling of a woman by her husband:

> *Husbands, likewise, dwell with them with understanding,*
> *giving honor to the wife, as to the weaker vessel, and as being*

heirs together of the grace of life, that your prayers may not
be hindered. (1 Peter 3:7 NKJV)

Wait a minute. Why should we honor that which is weak? We usually despise what is weak. If we accurately study this Scripture, we will find the emphasis is on not the weakness of the vessel, but on what's inside. What is a vessel anyway if not a container? The contents of this refined vase or vessel are what should be given due honor. The verse could be accurately rephrased as "Even though your wife is weaker physically, she is an equal heir of the grace of life." It is as though God is warning the men to be tender because if the women show up chipped and broken, there will be an issue between God, the men, and their prayers.

This verse is not so much about women being wimpy, weak, and on the verge of fainting as it is about treatment and honor. The woman is to be handled as more fragile because

> *Authentic women are not hard and calloused; they are tender and break easily.*

of the additional refinement of her nature. The man was from the dirt, and the woman was from the refined dirt of the man. This usually means men will "bounce" a bit better than women. I like to think of men as clay and women as crystal. I may not be totally accurate on this, but I still like to at least think it. It also tells us authentic women are not hard and calloused; they are tender and break easily. And of course each woman can increase her value by developing a noble character, and then she will excel the worth of rubies.

The Flawed Person Is Authentic

Because there is increased value tied to items that are authentic, they tend to be a bit more costly, just as crystal is more expensive than glass. Also, as we all know, expensive items often require some level of sacrifice to acquire.

In order to afford the purchase price of my diamond engagement ring, my husband, John, ate a diet of predominantly potatoes for two months. This sacrifice on his part was prompted after my response to a question John had posed early on in the ring search.

We were standing outside a jewelry store, looking at their display case and admiring the various cuts and sizes of the diamond engagement rings before we went in. I had pointed out a few I liked that seemed to be running consistently on the larger and more unusual side than the ones John gravitated toward. Finally, John stopped hinting and just put it out there.

"Which do you like better—the half-carat or the one-carat diamonds? I think the one-carat diamonds look too big."

There was not a moment of hesitation on my part. "I definitely like the one-carat better!"

We went into the store, and after we had priced the one-carat diamond rings, I could tell John was discouraged. They cost way more money than he had budgeted.

I figured I had said more than enough about my preferences, and right then and there I told him I would love whatever he gave me and suggested we not look at diamonds together anymore. I really preferred to just be surprised.

That night, John made a decision. There was no way he wasn't going to get me a one-carat diamond, and he immediately mapped out a plan to achieve this. He started calling diamond wholesalers.

He proposed on my birthday. Probably because he had no money for a birthday gift. He was so excited about giving me the ring, and I was totally shocked! Later we went to his apartment, where he showed me the appraisal of the diamond. The certified document specified the diamond's cut, color, and clarity.

It was official. In fact, I had an authentic diamond, but the fact it was genuine did not mean it was free of flaws. Actually, it is extremely rare for a genuine diamond to be graded as flawless. Most diamonds have at least slight flaws, and *these flaws actually authenticate the stone.* John showed me my diamond's visible flaws, which appeared as carbon shadows near the stone's point.

This should translate into good news for all of us: *To be authentic or genuine, we don't have to be flawless!* Our flaws actually declare us authentic. In fact, if we represent ourselves as flawless, then we most certainly declare ourselves as fake. No one is perfect or good, save God.

Why Flawed Is Better

Of course, if flawed and authentic is not your thing, there is another option. Something perfect and flawless awaits your purchase. You can buy a CZ, or cubic zirconia. They are abundant, man-made, flawless, and did I mention . . . cheap? These stones are not mined from the earth's depths, where heat and pressure have had their way. They are created in the sterile, controlled atmosphere of a laboratory. You can have a *real* CZ, but it would be a mistake to call a CZ "genuine" or "authentic." I know they might refer to it as such on a home shopping network. A real CZ is actually a fake diamond. You could set the CZ in a ring of gold and wear it as a diamond, and most would be none the wiser. But if you bought what you thought was a diamond only to later discover it was a CZ, you would definitely have been cheated. The fact that it was flawless would do little to compensate for the fact that it had no true value.

The untrained naked eye cannot differentiate between a CZ and a diamond because the difference is not immediately obvious. Only someone with a trained eye can tell the difference.

As a case in point, John returned from the Philippines with a gift to pass on to me. It *appeared* to be a ruby ring and earrings. The giver assured John they were genuine, but we both had our doubts. We accepted the gift as kind and thoughtful, regardless of the authenticity of the stones. The time came when I wanted to pass the jewelry on to someone else as a gift. It was then that I needed to know the truth.

There is a jeweler by the hair salon I frequent, so one day I took the ring in to the gemologist and asked her what she thought. As she handled the ring she shook her head doubtfully, but under the microscope all doubt was removed. Not only was it not a genuine ruby, it was a really bad fake. Magnified, I discovered, it was filled with all sorts of air bubbles. She commented that it looked rather like some child's science experiment. I could still give it to someone, but I would never dream of telling them it was genuine. It would have to be given as costume jewelry.

Under magnification and the scrutiny of intense light, we might find false perfection, bad imitations, or flaws revealed. It is always better to be a flawed authentic than to represent yourself as perfect and therefore a fake.

I think for a long time Christian women felt unreasonably pressured to appear perfect. This caused a lot of us to be both unapproachable and not genuine. It made others feel flawed and uncomfortable in our flashy CZ presence. In our pretense we all became white noise, and no one could hear what we had to say through all the surface conversation. We foolishly imagined pretending to be perfect would inspire perfection, but rather than lifting others up, we weighed them down.

Authentic. The term *authentic* is used to describe something genuine and original, as opposed to something that is fake or a reproduction. An authentic item is legally valid. This would mean the authentic would not be *the forced,* but *the forged* in your life. I like to think of it as flaws encased in beauty and light.

The definition of *real* does not go as deep. *Real* is first defined as merely having actual physical existence.

God is looking for genuine authenticity in His daughters. He invites us to reflect the beauty and the price paid for our salvation; to be His gemstones who have allowed their flaws to be set in stones of light and fire. *Real* is tied to fact, but *authentic* and *genuine* are tied to truth and process.

When John Keats wrote about the relationship between truth and beauty, I can't imagine he ever thought beauty would be pursued independent of truth. In clearer times, as one sought truth he discovered beauty abiding in its presence. If Keats is correct and these two are in fact intertwined, what do we find when we pursue beauty outside the realm of truth?

Perhaps this is best illustrated in our lives today. I believe our culture has chosen to pursue beauty from the perspective of reality rather than from the realm of truth. It would be difficult to find poetic harmony in the words "Beauty is reality; reality is beauty." Why? Because it is just not true. Reality is rarely a thing of beauty, and for most elements of life, beauty is not a reality. Keats could tie beauty to truth because truth is ultimately tied to the nature of God, which makes it not only beautiful but unshakable. Reality is fleeting and therefore tied to only the season or the moment.

In order to gain a better understanding, we should discuss some terms. First, there is the word *truth*. Its definitions include the words *honesty, sincerity, integrity,* and *faithfulness.* As we look around, we find truth a rare commodity. Whenever truth is revealed, it begs a decision of us. Do we embrace it and change, or do we turn toward the comfort of a less-confrontational lie? Only truth stops the progression of a lie.

There has never been a more desperate need for beauty and truth. People everywhere are discouraged. They don't know what to believe anymore. There has been a constant barrage of lies on almost every front and undermining every level of life. These lies have produced widespread disappointment, and many have given up their quest for truth and settled instead for reality. Never confuse reality with truth. Truth is foundational, while reality is unstable at best.

Reality morphs into the image of its surroundings and adapts to its culture and time, while truth stands unmoved by cultural influences. Truth remains an absolute, which rightfully invites our culture to embrace the foundation of its wisdom. Reality holds up the standard of *what is,* while truth lifts the banner of *what could be.* The counsel of reality foolishly encourages us to accept what is as the way things will always be.

The revelation of truth awakens the hope of something so much more. Reality reasons that everyone lies and puts their spin on things . . . that's just the way it is. Accepting this reality as truth gives us permission on some level to go ahead and lie. The voice of wisdom refuses to accept reality as truth and challenges us all to rise above the norm, encouraging us to speak differently. Wisdom admonishes us in the book of Proverbs,

> *I speak the truth and hate every kind of deception. My advice is wholesome and good. There is nothing crooked or twisted in it. My words are plain to anyone with understanding, clear to those who want to learn.*   (8:7–9 NLT)

A Heart Connection

As I travel to speak at or attend conferences, I have an opportunity to connect on a more personal level with women. I have found that women hear my message in many different ways. They might hear what I say on the level of mental instruction. My message will be received as information on the basis of merit. Have they heard it before, did I make logical sense, etc. If I pass the test, my words will be processed along with all the other information they have stored mentally.

Everything is processed analytically, and more often than not they're listening for me to make a mistake. Often this is done for personal safety reasons. It is a head-to-head connection. Truthfully, I have found that when people listen to me expecting me to make a mistake or say something stupid, I never disappoint them.

Another way they may hear me speak to them is on the level of personality. This is when they hear what I say and process it emotionally. They embrace my words if they admire me or connect with my personality. It could be they find me entertaining, and this connection is driven more often than not by whether I inspire them and hold their attention emotionally . . . it is a soul-to-soul connection.

Then there is the deepest and most lasting connection, the heart connection. This occurs when you sit in the audience and feel as though the speaker is bringing life and words to your unspoken thoughts and longings. Perhaps they are saying publicly the very things God has whispered to you in secret. You are not only there mentally and emotionally; the connection runs much deeper. You are connected because you resonate in your spirit with what is being said. You might not even like the way the speaker is dressed, the way he or she talks, or the outline of their presentation. You may have noted a few errors, but when there is a connection, none of these things interfere because you've already gone underground to the heart. On the deepest level, nothing in the presentation matters as much as what is being said. When I have had this kind of connection in a service I often hear the Spirit speak things to me that are ignited by something else the speaker said.

The first level is an intellectual, informational connection. The second is an emotional or personality connection. The third is a spirit and heart connection. Of course, you can and will connect with people on all three levels. All levels are healthy and necessary, but the deepest work and awakening happens when there is a heart connection. Reality does not make this deep connection . . . but truth and beauty do.

This Earth Is Not Enough

It is not going to be enough to be real. We must move beyond what has been and cry out for the restoration of the beauty of truth. We see this theme repeated in King David's life. His life comparisons sound like this: "God, in reality this is what I have, but truthfully I long for this." David repeatedly declared God's truth preeminent over his current reality.

Though an army besiege me, my heart will not fear; though war break out against me, even then will I be confident. One

> *thing I ask of the* LORD, *this is what I seek: that I may dwell*
> *in the house of the* LORD *all the days of my life, to gaze upon*
> *the beauty of the* LORD.   (Psalm 27:3–4 NIV)

David's reality was a life filled with war and enemies both within and without, yet in the midst of it all, God was more than enough. Somehow David was able to glimpse beyond the vapor of this world and find himself positioned in the realm of truth on the other side in a place of peace and unfathomable beauty.

What we have is not what we long to embrace. What we see is not what we look for. What we hear is not the song our hearts sing.

The fragrances of earth entice but fail to transport us. What we drink does not quench our recurring thirst. What we eat does not long satiate our gnawing hunger. The seed of eternity was planted within us, and nothing of this earth will ever truly satisfy. Earth's bounty and beauty were given only to ignite our appetite for something so much more.

We cry out for more than the real—we are desperate for the enduring and authentic.

Part of being authentic is realizing the value of the original. Originals are the beginning of something. An example of an original is a genuine work of art, not a copy or a forgery. Do you realize there is something extremely unique and original about you? You need to be true to who God forged you to be.

For example, I hate panty hose. I think they are evil. I seriously have to wonder if they are not a major health risk and the reason behind cellulite. So I don't wear them. If someone else thinks panty hose are healthy and helpful, more power to them. They should not stop wearing them because of me. But if someone thinks panty hose are godly, then a question of Christian conformity arises. Panty hose are not godly or ungodly; they are just really tight, stretchy stuff that enwraps your legs. I'm glad that's settled.

Whether you embrace your uniqueness or live out your life as only a

mixed forgery of the lives of others is really up to you. But know this:
The whole world is watching in the hope that you will be an original.

———————

Heavenly Father,

*I come to You in the name of Jesus. I want to be a diamond, not a CZ.
I want to be flawed but authentic. I want to walk this life consistently
in all settings. Father, forgive me for the times I was real or just real
carnal. When I lashed out at those who hurt or maligned me. I choose
to bless those who curse me and do good to those who've used or abused
me. Amen.*

———————

CHAPTER THIRTEEN

Fighting with Accessories

I've always liked stones. I had a passion for rock collecting when I was a child. My friend Marci and I would scan creek bottoms and sort through yards of pea gravel wherever we found it. I remember sitting for hours as we sifted through the gravel that would form my next-door neighbor's future driveway. We searched in the sunshine of a summer's afternoon, hoping to find Indian beads. And find them we did. We were on a mission to rescue these lost relics before they were encased under a layer of blacktop and lost for all time.

When I was young, walks were treasure hunts. I scanned streets and vacant lots for rocks and arrowheads. I dug in my yard and sifted through our landscaping rocks for fossils, mica, fool's gold, and agates. I saved my money and purchased Apache Tears and pink-lace agates at rock shows.

My treasure hunting was not limited to stones. One summer I spent hours digging my toes into the muddy depths of Lake Freeman. I was searching for lake mussels. I knew a pearl was hidden among one of them. I transferred my victims from the dock into an old paint bucket and convinced my father they should be brought home as pets. I imagined myself feeding these bumpy mussels a steady diet of sand, and in return they would give me a magnificent pearl. It wasn't long before they died off. Somehow I was able to convince my father to check each one for a pearl before he tossed the stinky mess. Overcome with guilt and barely able to stomach the smell, I watched from a distance. I sat on the back stoop as my father used his old Navy knife to scrape each one clean before discarding it. While he cleaned the mussels, he told me stories of oysters and the female Japanese pearl divers. I imagined them as brave mermaids who plunged fearlessly into the deep in order to bring its hidden treasures to the surface. They dived for those who could not hold their breath.

I wanted to visit the ocean floor and borrow its beauty. I was not as interested in keeping the pearl as I was in the thrill of discovery. As he talked, my father's knife struck something hard in the flesh of a mussel. It was a pearl! It was about the size of a nickel—flat and odd-shaped, but it was a pearl no less! I was beside myself with joy. I knew there was beauty to be found amid my stinky mussels if we only looked hard enough.

Finding the Rare Amid the Ordinary

One of my sons seems to have inherited my fantasy of finding rare beauty amid the ordinary. John and I were out of town for our annual board meeting when we received an excited call from home. It was then ten-year-old Alec, breathlessly explaining how he had just made thirty dollars. It seems in our absence Alec had dug rocks out of our backyard, run them through the dishwasher, and then sold them to our neighbors from a stand he set up at the end of our driveway. The temperature had dropped below freezing, and I am sure my neighbors were intrigued to find an entrepreneur in the bitter cold of a Colorado January. One kind soul had listened intently as Alec explained his most prized stone. The man purchased it from him for thirty dollars. I was stunned, but before I could make a comment I heard Alec sigh remorsefully.

"Mom, I really should have sold it for more . . . I think it had a sapphire inside it."

What a gift to be able to see something of beauty hidden within something so rough and common. I ask you, does our Father see us any differently?

When we hung up the phone, John and I shook our heads and laughed out loud. Alec is so free from this world's paradigm. He was looking for the beauty within and would not be convinced it was not there.

Time passed, and we bought Alec a rock polisher for Christmas. It consisted of a tumbler, rough stones, polishing mediums, and some accessories for setting the finished stones.

Let the unaware be warned: A rock polisher is a time-and-noise commitment. First, you put the rocks in with one polishing medium, plug the thing in, and let it tumble for a few weeks before adding the second, finer medium, and then the process begins again. There were many times when, alone in our quiet house, I would experience a momentary feeling of panic . . . *What is that noise coming from the basement?* Then I would remember . . . *It's the rock polisher.* I became anxious for the process to be over—why did it have to take so long? I would question Alec and John, but they assured me it wasn't yet time to release the rocks.

Finally the big day came. There seemed to be a bit of concern about where we could dump the polishing medium; it couldn't go down the drain or in the yard. Double-bagging and straight out to the garbage was the only answer. There was a lot of scurrying and rinsing, and then the rocks emerged. They were shiny, smooth, and shockingly smaller versions of the stones we had put in. There was one in particular that caught my notice. Weeks ago it had gone into the polisher a dusty, rough-looking piece of amethyst, and now it was a small, shiny purple pebble. As I turned it in my hand to feel all the sides of its cool smoothness, I sensed the Holy Spirit speaking to me:

The stone you hold is the same chemical and molecular compound as an amethyst gemstone, but it differs vastly in value. This one cannot be set as jewelry, for it has no edges, facets, or fire. It is not unlike My children. There are those who go through the same process over and over again, until all their edges are dulled by the repeated experience. I love them and they are Mine, but how I long to recapture their fire, to give them facets, clean lines, and the beauty of captured light.

It was so true; the greatest difference between the purple stone in my hand and an amethyst set in a ring was in the method of preparation and processing. I've found myself meditating on the comparison ever since.

A Thirst for Fire

There is something amazing about any stone that captures light. As I have grown older, I have developed a decided preference for the fire of gemstones. Their beauty is not mine for the digging. They are costly. I have lived long enough to discover that everything of beauty in my life has been birthed through the process of fire or severe cutting.

> *Everything of beauty in my life has been birthed through the process of fire.*

There have been many areas and lessons in my life where God wanted to produce a jewel, and I allowed Him access to only the rock-polisher dynamic. Instead of surrendering, I whined and complained that life (He) wasn't fair! There were times I drew back when He invited me to come a bit closer. Other times, I clung to relationships He asked me to sever. In those seasons there was the constant hum of the rock polisher in my life. It turned around and around as I resisted the beauty that could have been realized in an instant of total surrender and obedience.

The truth is, most women like jewels and jewelry. We are supposed to.

Before you get all excited and begin to quote passages out of the book of 1 Peter, listen with your heart. I did not say we are to *lust* after jewelry or trust in our accessories as an accurate measure of our worth; but rather each daughter has a God-given appreciation for the beauty of jewels. Why else would God hide such a multitude of various and precious stones within the earth if not for His children to unearth and enjoy?

But what good is a stone without a setting?

Throughout God's Word we find references to precious stones. God instructed skilled craftsmen to construct a square breastplate for Aaron and place twelve precious stones in it to represent each of the tribes of Israel.

> *Then they mounted four rows of precious stones on it. In the first row there was a ruby, a topaz and a beryl; in the second row a turquoise, a sapphire and an emerald; in the third row a jacinth, an agate and an amethyst; in the fourth row a chrysolite, an onyx and a jasper. They were mounted in gold filigree settings. There were twelve stones, one for each of the names of the sons of Israel.* (Exodus 39:10–14 NIV)

These stones were not superglued onto the fabric; each was carefully secured in a setting of gold filigree. This representation declared each tribe not only precious but unique in His sight. As His children, I believe, this is how He chooses to see us. The book of Malachi describes God's attachment to His people this way:

> *"They shall be Mine," says the LORD of hosts, "on the day that I make them My jewels. And I will spare them as a man spares his own son who serves him." Then you shall again discern between the righteous and the wicked, between one who serves God and one who does not serve Him.*
>
> (3:17-18 NKJV)

How does God make us His jewels? I believe this comes by a revelation of light and fire.

> *I will bring that group through the fire and make them pure,*
> *just as gold and silver are refined and purified by fire. They*
> *will call on my name, and I will answer them. I will say,*
> *"These are my people," and they will say, "The LORD is our*
> *God."* (Zechariah 13:9 NLT)

Fire makes us pure. Fire separates the precious from the vile and makes the hidden apparent. When silver is heated to such an extreme temperature that it becomes liquid, any dross in the metal rises to the surface. As our impurities bubble up and dance on the surface, there is a decision to be made: Do we leave them or

> *Who you are in the fire is who you are.*

let them be removed? If we choose to allow the dross or impurities to remain in the metal of our lives, they will become invisible again as the furnace cools down. This revelation of fire usually will occur in the secret place of your heart. Often we will be in prayer when God points out these impurities.

Fire Reveals the Authentic

I don't really like this truth, but here it is anyway: Who you are in the fire is who you are. I want to imagine that who I am on television is the true representation of who I am. I like the edited version of me. I like how I look after an hour with a makeup artist and someone who actually knows how to style my hair. I like kind lighting, a controlled set, and a clapping audience, but none of these dynamics reveal my hidden flaws. These usually come out when some area of my life is crossed.

*Behold, I have refined you, but not as silver; I have tested you
in the furnace of affliction.*   (Isaiah 48:10 NKJV)

I would have loved it if God had rephrased some of this. "I have tested you in the sauna of the spa experience" would have been nice.

In the book of Esther, we read: "Before a girl's turn came to go in to King Xerxes, she had to complete twelve months of beauty treatments" (2:12 NIV). I have told my husband he would have an Esther too if I could go through a year's worth of beauty treatments. But alas, just like Esther we are not defined by who we are in the spa. We are defined by who we are in the fire. Esther was tested before she ever entered the yearlong spa, and she repeatedly chose obedience. Fire definitely reveals our flaws, but if we let it have its work in us, it reveals something lovely as well.

One weekend John was scheduled to speak at a conference and two churches in the San Diego area. This presented an opportunity for two of my sons and me to join him. We left Colorado Springs very early in the morning and flew to California, only to discover that our hotel room would not be available for another six to eight hours.

John rushed off to his meeting, and we were left to make the best of our time while waiting for the room. It was raining, so we wandered in and out of stores in an attempt to stay dry and stave off boredom. One of these was a jewelry store filled with all sorts of fun silver jewelry. I picked out a blue topaz ring that I really liked and tried it on for fun. It was a perfect fit. It could replace a topaz ring that I had managed to knock the stone out of. I returned it to the salesclerk and decided I would bring John back to store when he was finished with his speaking engagement and show it to him.

When John joined us a few hours later, I asked him if he was interested in buying me a ring. After all, our twenty-first anniversary was less than a month away, and he was not even going to be with me; he would be "down under" in Australia. Didn't he want me to have something special to look at while he was gone? (Yes, I was cashing in.) He agreed to look at the ring, and after lunch we all returned to the store. The storeowner saw me coming and pulled out the ring. I slipped it on and modeled it for John.

"See how well it fits? It could replace the ring with the lost stone and be my anniversary gift."

"How much is it?" John asked.

"Forty-five dollars," the clerk replied.

"Sure, we'll take it," John said, closing the deal.

I fought a moment of panic. Forty-five dollars? It probably wasn't even real. I had sold out very cheaply for my twenty-first-anniversary present!

While I paid for it, John decided to take our two boys outside.

Now that I had the shop owner in private, I decided to ask her about the authenticity of the stone.

"Is this a genuine blue topaz?" I probed.

"There is no such thing as a genuine blue topaz," she answered.

Now I was even more confused.

"But I've seen them," I said, fearful I'd just purchased a piece of aqua glass.

"All topaz is brown until you put it in the fire," she explained. "Their color comes out in the heat."

She shared how a brown vein of tanzanite was transformed into beautiful blues and purples after an encounter with lightning. She explained how precious stones were born of fire.

"So it's not fake?" I asked again.

"It's as genuine as a blue topaz can be," she assured me.

Fire does not just reveal what is flawed; it reveals what is beautiful as well. Who would have imagined colors ranging from the aqua of water to the blue of the sky could be coaxed from brown?

Beauty in the Dark

Many years ago I was given a portion of an amethyst geode. The outside is gnarled and rusty. Looking at it, you would never guess that it encased pristine purple crystal formations. Nothing on the outside of the geode betrays even a hint of the beauty on the inside. The outside tells the story of the heat and the pressure, but the inside reveals what beauty has been born of this encounter with fire.

Most gemstones are mined. This means they are forged in a hidden environment of pressure before they are ever unearthed and brought into the light.

I love the beautiful example of gems found in the Christian classic *Hinds' Feet on High Places*. As the story progresses, Much Afraid is repeatedly given opportunity to make altars of obedience and surrender to the Shepherd. Each time her sacrifice is consumed, a stone is revealed in the midst of the ashes. These stones look common and ordinary, but she keeps them in her bag as a reminder of the lesson learned. There is a time of great discouragement when Much Afraid is tempted to discard the common rocks and thinks herself foolish for retaining what appears to be worthless. It is only later that she discovers each to be a gem.

There is something of beauty to be learned from every dark and lonely place in our lives. It is in those times of obedience during suffering that we have an opportunity to experience our Father as more than enough. Out of the rough material of our trials, He is more than willing to fashion objects of beauty.

Even the most magnificent jewels, such as the Star of India or the Hope Diamond, were once humble pieces of carbon. These misshaped stones were skillfully transformed into beautiful gems. To accomplish this they had to be cut, faceted, and polished. During the gem cutting, a substantial amount of stone can be lost. Often only 20 percent of the rough gem's original weight will be saved. It all depends on what the jeweler is looking for. Does he want a smaller gem with better clarity or a larger one with less? When the whole process is complete, it is hard to believe the small, symmetrical, sparkling gem of fire was born from a rough, lopsided stone. This is similar to the very wonder of what God longs to do in us.

How We Become Jewels

I delight greatly in the LORD; my soul rejoices in my God. For he has clothed me with garments of salvation and arrayed me in a robe of righteousness, as a bridegroom adorns his head like a priest, and as a bride adorns herself with her jewels. (Isaiah 61:10 NIV)

Brides are to adorn themselves with jewels. These accessories are presented to us as we obey during our times of suffering. It is this process that reveals the beauty and sets stones of value in mountings of filigree.

Look back over the past year. Have you been shorting yourself of beautiful long-term accessories because you were afraid of the process required to receive them? Maybe you endured the process but have been complaining the whole way through and now fear you will end up with a key chain rather than a necklace. Or perhaps you already have a collection of jewels and do not even know it.

The Bible tells us that Jesus for the joy set before Him endured the Cross. In our trials, large or small, it is crucial that we allow joy to be set before us. Can you believe He is ready to take the pain and frustration and make it an object of beauty? Let's pray together,

———

Heavenly Father,

I come to You in the name of Jesus. By the power of Your Holy Spirit, I ask You to take the rocks in my life and make them objects of beauty.

Forgive me for any murmuring and complaining. I want to come out of the rock polisher. Father, have Your way. Purify me and bring out my unique color with Your holy fire. Facet my life and position me in the setting of Your choice. Give me Your eyes to see and Your promise of beauty and strength in every process and season of life. Amen.

———

CHAPTER FOURTEEN

Fighting with Influence

A prophetess named Deborah, the wife of Lappidoth, was judge of Israel at that time. Deborah would sit under the Palm Tree of Deborah, which was between the cities of Ramah and Bethel, in the mountains of Ephraim. And the people of Israel would come to her to settle their arguments. (Judges 4:4-5 NCV)

This sounds like a sweet job, one I just might enjoy—being a prophetess who sits under a palm tree passing judgment. I can imagine it all so clearly: I would hold court on silken pillows under the shade of a stately palm named after me. I'd be seen reclining patiently, while my people brought their disputes before me and I dispensed God-given wisdom. I rather think with four sons (three of whom are teens!), I have had adequate preparation for just such a role.

My résumé of experience would also encompass the many times I've passed judgment on disputes that often had nothing to do with me, such as those involving my friends or blood relatives. I've tried to cut this activity back since encountering the truth that the measure we use to judge is the measure by which we will be judged.

Yes, at first I imagined I could definitely be anointed to sip lemonade and regally listen, buoyed by the assurance that the people who came actually had to not only listen to but also obey my directives. I would be the ultimate big boss, which is definitely not always the case at my house.

In all seriousness, though, I and possibly other women may have romanticized Deborah's role and even wondered what could happen if we were given the chance to be in charge. As I studied further I discovered this fantasy was a far cry from Deborah's reality. After all, no one ever makes history by just sitting around and judging. I believe Deborah's life and circumstances hold an urgent message and awakening for the women of our age.

Life After Ehud

We often read Bible stories already knowing the end, and therefore find it difficult to truly immerse ourselves in the life struggles or realities of these heroes of faith. Their struggles were very real, their fears not so different from our own. Likewise, their prayers, dreams, and hopes for their children paralleled ours. Let's step back a verse or two and find out why Deborah was in power and what type of domain and spiritual climate she actually inherited.

> *After Ehud died, the Israelites again did what the LORD said was wrong.* (Judges 4:1 NCV)

Ehud was judge before Deborah, and with his death everything changed. First, we must know who Ehud was in his season of time. He judged Israel for eighty years and began his tenure by aggressively confronting and pushing back their enemies. Under his leadership, they pushed back Moab, killing ten thousand able-bodied men in the process. This victory so inspired one brother, Shamgar, that he went on to kill six hundred Philistine men with an ox goad, which could best be described as an intimidating stick. This would not necessarily have been my weapon of choice, but it does illustrate this major point: *When God is with you, it really doesn't matter what is in your hand . . . only that you use it.* With the momentum of this victory and the reestablishment of healthy

> When God is with you, it really doesn't matter what is in your hand . . . only that you use it.

boundaries and borders, the nation rested for eight decades, which means there were those who lived and died and never knew battle. Often this is when we're the most vulnerable—when all is at rest.

As time passed, the people forgot the reasons why they had enjoyed nearly a century of peace when surrounded by enemies. Perhaps they even forgot what had gotten them into trouble in the first place. Or maybe they just thought God didn't mind the way they lived. Maybe they thought God's season of involvement was over, and they could handle it from there. After all, they were His chosen ones. Wasn't He for them no matter what? If they got into any trouble, surely a good ox goad could fix it. So they honored the passing of their beloved judge Ehud by returning almost immediately to what the Lord said was *wrong*. We read the word *again,* meaning this was not the first time the Israelites had blown it!

Now, I understand in our politically correct, sensitive, and tolerant society, *wrong* is a bad word. It implies that there just might be a *right,* which is a rather frightening aspect to most of us because we have decided to place everything (including murder) under the right of personal preference or decision. What is right for you may be wrong for me, and what is wrong for you may be right for me . . . No wonder so many are confused. Our present society aside, God had very definite ideas of what was wrong, and He responded accordingly.

So he let Jabin, a king of Canaan who ruled in the city of Hazor, defeat Israel. Sisera, who lived in Harosheth Hag-

goyim, was the commander of Jabin's army. Because he had
nine hundred iron chariots and was very cruel to the people
of Israel for twenty years, they cried to the LORD for help.

(Judges 4:2–3 NCV)

In response, God let Jabin, the ruler of Canaan, defeat His people. Notice the use of the word *let,* which of course is a permissive word that implies God *allowed* Jabin access to this victory. And as if this humiliation were not enough, He turned the people over to the marshal law of a general named Sisera, who was not just cruel, but *very cruel* with his nine hundred iron chariots. (Suddenly, wielding the ox goad felt a bit silly.) Overwhelmed by the odds against them, God's people began to cry out once again for His help. Actually, to be exact, they wailed for twenty years.

Enter Deborah

This is the kind of oppressive, hopeless atmosphere Deborah inherited and found herself presiding judge and prophetess over—rather bleak, to say the least. Then there is the question of why the weight of all this fell upon the shoulders of a woman. Perhaps all the men of power and influence had been run down by iron chariots at the pleasure of the twisted and perverse General Sisera. Maybe he made a mockery of the Israelites by allowing them only a woman to lead them. Or he might not even have noticed or acknowledged her as a leader. After all, what can one woman sitting in the middle of nowhere do? Obviously, a lot.

Yes, the people had foolishly chosen to do wrong, and now they were crying. And Deborah found herself poised between two brokenhearted cities without even a building in which to hold court. There was only a palm, the Palm of Deborah. This was her place and the only oasis of hope from injustice and oppression on a dusty road between two cities. The walls of protection were torn down, and the villages no longer prospered. Not only were things bad *for* Israel, things were bad *in* Israel. There was conflict within as well as oppression and violence without. There was infighting among God's people.

We know this to be true because Deborah spent her time settling the arguments of God's people. She didn't spend her time mediating on Israel's behalf by complaining about injustices or legislating relational boundaries with Sisera in the Canaan courts. I doubt she even had a position of influence in these courts. As a judge, her time was spent navigating the conflicts of her own people, Israel. She settled disputes in an attempt to keep the children of God from biting, devouring, and suing one another.

As prophetess, she was God's voice to His disobedient children. She was both their correction and their comfort. The name Deborah means "honeybee." I am certain she often felt as though she had been placed in a hive of buzzing turmoil while she listened to complaints, all the while trying to derive something sweet and sustaining from God's word for her people. This unrest might have been all the children of Israel dared hope for; after all, they had been faithless.

But this was all was about to change. The day came when she was no longer content to sit and judge the conflicts among her own, to watch the hopeless infighting while a harsh and cruel enemy mocked their God and ravaged their cities. She had grown weary of the sound of mourning and despair and chose instead to sing.

The Song of Deborah says a day came when she arose and summoned a sleeping warrior named Barak. As she did so, she left behind her former posture and position of twenty years. There would be no turning back. No more waiting passively for conflict and atrocities to come her way. She'd had enough. She was tired of waiting for something more while mediating conflict . . . it was time to take the battle to the enemy. Other translations variously precede the Scripture below with "Now," "One day," or even "Then." It is always interesting to examine this element of timing. I want to ask, Why then? Why not twenty years earlier? What was she waiting for?

Deborah sent a message to Barak son of Abinoam. Barak
lived in the city of Kedesh, which is in the area of Naphtali.

(Judges 4:6 NCV)

Barak lived in a city of refuge named Kedesh. It is interesting that his name literally means "lightning." God was preparing to strike out suddenly from a city of frightened refugees.

Deborah said to Barak, "The LORD, the God of Israel, com-
mands you: 'Go and gather ten thousand men of Naphtali
and Zebulun and lead them to Mount Tabor.'"

(Judges 4:6 NCV)

I am amazed at the strength of this directive. It is definitely not like the ones we usually hear, which are more like prayer suggestions, such as "I was praying about this, and I thought you might want to consider gathering a couple thousand men, and maybe Mount Tabor would be a convenient location for everyone." No, she totally removed herself, her opinion, and any question from the equation. She had heard the word of the Lord, and her only responsibility was to relay it.

Whenever God begins to shift things, there is a sense of urgency. He appears to respond to our desperate prayers or outcries with a sudden move from inaction to action and interrupts our cycle of despair. If we are wise, we will allow this urgency to carry over to our responses and obedience to His call to action.

Historically, the need for immediate obedience encourages hidden leaders to come forth, gather the discouraged warriors, and equip them with the assurance of God's victory. Deborah's message in fact stirs Barak. The people are excited. God is going to fight for them again and rout their enemies as in the days of old! God has promised that if Barak will gather and lead this assembly, He will do the rest.

I will make Sisera, the commander of Jabin's army, and his chariots, and his army meet you at the Kishon River. I will hand Sisera over to you.   (Judges 4:7 NCV)

This sounds like it was a done deal. Sisera, his army, and all the dreaded chariots would be turned over to Barak. The time had come for the cruel and mighty to surrender to the weak and oppressed. You would think he would jump all over this, but Barak hesitated. Why? God's command and promise stirred him enough to respond, but not enough to move him into action. He was afraid. Twenty years as a refugee had taken their toll, and even with ten thousand men he would not face Sisera unless Deborah went with him. He went to Deborah with this reply:

I will go if you will go with me, but if you won't go with me, I won't go.   (Judges 4:8 NCV)

Let's step back a minute and really process his response. Of course, it is very telling of the climate of the time. Here is a man so beaten down and discouraged, he has forgotten his name. A guy with a name that means "lightning" should not be afraid of anything or anyone; he should just be poised and ready to strike. I imagine Deborah heard God say it more like this,

Lightning, The LORD, the God of Israel, commands you: Go and gather ten thousand men!   (Judges 4:9)

This has a whole different feel to it. It is hard to imagine *lightning* thinking it needs a *honeybee* to keep it company. Even more than asking her to go with him, he refused to go without her. He actually threatened to disobey the command of both his earthly ruler and his heavenly Ruler if she did not accompany him. This shows how discouraged the men of this time were.

"Of course I will go with you," Deborah answered, "but you
will not get credit for the victory. The LORD will let a woman
defeat Sisera." So Deborah went with Barak to Kedesh.

(Judges 4:9 NCV)

Deborah readily agreed to go along, but explained that even before
the battle began he would lose personal credit for his victory to a
woman. I love that Deborah used her authority and influence to foster
obedience in Barak. She did not try to pull her rank as a judge, or play
her "God card" as prophetess and rebuke him for his defiance. She lent
him her strength.

All true leaders, whether male or female, need to lend their strength
rather than pull rank. When children are frightened, sometimes they just
need someone to walk them up the
stairs. It is not always about doing it
alone, but it is always about doing it.
If you didn't read this story all the
way through, you might be tempted
to think Deborah was referring to
gaining credit for the defeat of Sisera

> *All true leaders, whether*
> *male or female, need to*
> *lend their strength*
> *rather than pull rank.*

for herself, but she was not. Another woman soon to come on the scene,
Jael, would finish the job.

The Enemy Declawed

Deborah arose and accompanied Barak to Kedesh, where they called together the ten thousand men from Naphtali and Zebulun. While all this
was happening, a spy named Heber reported their gathering to Sisera.

When Sisera was told that Barak son of Abinoam had gone to
Mount Tabor, Sisera gathered his nine hundred iron chariots
and all the men with him, from Harosheth Haggoyim to the
Kishon River. (Judges 4:12 NCV)

Imagine the terror the Israelites must have initially felt: *Oh, no; the enemy found out what we were going to do, and he has come out in full force to crush us!* But I love the way God works. Sisera thought he was on his way to put down an uprising, only to meet his downfall. What he thought was secret intelligence was actually God's lure, which means God can use even a gossip to draw the enemy into defeat. Deborah had already seen this in the Spirit, and instead of being intimidated, she knew the enemy's army was all present and accounted for—which could mean only one thing: It was time!

> *Then Deborah said to Barak, "Get up! Today is the day the* Lord *will hand over Sisera. The* Lord *has already cleared the way for you." So Barak led ten thousand men down Mount Tabor.*
> (Judges 4:14 NCV)

Barak and his men were surrounded on Mount Tabor, and Deborah declared, "The Lord has already cleared the way for you." I wonder if that would have been my response. I fear my words would have reflected what I actually saw: "Oh, no! We're surrounded, and there is no way out!" rather than what God has promised, "I am handing them over to you." Perhaps Deborah's ability to see beyond the circumstances was the very reason Barak valued her company. For when the Deborahs, the women with prophetic vision, call, the princes arise. Watch what happened:

> *As Barak approached, the* Lord *confused Sisera and his army and chariots. The* Lord *defeated them with the sword, but Sisera left his chariot and ran away on foot.*
> (Judges 4:15 NCV)

I love this. It says that at the mere approach of Barak, Sisera, his army, and even the terrifying iron chariots were thrown into utter disarray. The children of Israel had only to unsheathe their swords, and the enemy was defeated and lost in confusion. Sisera appeared to be escaping, when actually he would meet his death in the tent of an ally.

Barak and his men chased Sisera's chariots and army to Harosheth Haggoyim. With their swords they killed all of Sisera's men; not one of them was left alive. Barak and his ten thousand progressed from merely approaching the enemy to victoriously engaging them, then shamelessly chasing them down.

> *But Sisera himself ran away to the tent where Jael lived. She was the wife of Heber, one of the Kenite family groups. Heber's family was at peace with Jabin king of Hazor.*
>
> (Judges 4:17 NCV)

Sisera ran to the tent of his ally Heber the Kenite. Heber had somehow managed to arrange peace with King Jabin, even though he should not have been able to, as Heber was a descendant of Jethro, Moses' father-in-law. I imagine Heber was still out of town, because he had just sold out Barak and was waiting a safe distance away until the battle was over. Sisera ran to this tent of alliance, thinking in it he would find safety. But when God begins to turn the tables, there is no safe place for the enemy.

> *Jael went out to meet Sisera and said to him, "Come into my tent, master! Come in. Don't be afraid." So Sisera went into Jael's tent, and she covered him with a rug.* (Judges 4:18 NCV)

Jael went out to meet him. It makes me think she heard the sound of God's approaching judgment and began to watch for her moment. She invited him in and covered him with a rug. This is reminiscent of Rahab the harlot in the book of Exodus, who switched allegiance when she hid the spies. But Jael was not hiding spies; she was hiding an enemy of God and she knew it. He was thirsty and asked for water, but she gave him milk instead. Why? She wanted to lull him to sleep. He drank and asked her to guard the door of the tent and tell any who might ask of his whereabouts that he was not there. She agreed, but only until he was lost in the deep sleep of utter exhaustion.

> But Jael, the wife of Heber, took a tent peg and a hammer and quietly went to Sisera. Since he was very tired, he was in a deep sleep. She hammered the tent peg through the side of Sisera's head and into the ground. And so Sisera died.
>
> (Judges 4:21 NCV)

A rather gory approach to assassination, to say the least, but there is a lesson for each of us in Jael's hammer and tent peg: God will always use what is in our hands. He will anoint what we have already been faithful to wield.

Remember, David would not fight in Saul's armor because he had yet to test or prove it. When facing an enemy is not the time to try a new technique or approach. You use what your hands have already found true and strong. What is in your hand?

> At that very moment Barak came by Jael's tent, chasing Sisera. Jael went out to meet him and said, "Come. I will show you the man you are looking for." So Barak entered her tent, and there Sisera lay dead, with the tent peg in his head.
>
> (Judges 4:22 NCV)

I love God's timing: "*At that very moment* Barak came by Jael's tent." How different the circumstances might have been if Jael had not already killed Sisera! In the heat of the moment she might have found her life forfeit for aiding and concealing an enemy of Israel. But, instead of being executed, she was exalted. She again went out to meet Barak and humbly showed him the enemy he was looking for—dead on her floor.

> On that day God defeated Jabin king of Canaan in the sight of Israel.   (Judges 4:23 NCV)

What? They didn't even meet Jabin on the battlefield that day, but God did. It was the day Jabin was pulled down from his lofty position and the shift of power began. Do you see this? Jabin was defeated first in the sight of the Israelites, and then at a later date he was utterly destroyed by them.

> *Israel became stronger and stronger against Jabin king of Canaan until finally they destroyed him.*   (Judges 4:24 NCV)

This Is Her Story; This Is Her Song

Battles are won in the realm of the spirit long before they are ever finalized in the natural. You must allow God to settle it while you are on your knees before you can get the strength to stand before an enemy. You have to see the enemy defeated before you will ever gain the strength necessary to win. With the realization that God was again fighting for them, the people of Israel no longer saw their enemy as intimidating and all-powerful.

I love this illustration because it has both a story and a song. The story gives the details and account of what transpired on earth, while the song lends us a glimpse of what happened in the heavenlies.

As New Testament Christians, we rarely war as God instructed the children of Israel to do, so this insight into the realm of the Spirit is essential.

> *For our struggle is not against flesh and blood, but against the rulers, against the authorities, against the powers of this dark world and against the spiritual forces of evil in the heavenly realms.*   (Ephesians 6:12 NIV)

This version certainly is a lot less gory than the tent peg and mallet approach.

The Song of Deborah

> There were no warriors in Israel
>> until I, Deborah, arose,
>> until I arose to be a mother to Israel . . .
> Wake up, wake up, Deborah!
>> Wake up, wake up, sing a song!
> Get up, Barak!
>> Go capture your enemies, son of Abinoam! (Judges 5:7, 12 NCV)

What do we see happening here? There were no warriors so a mother stood up? Is God getting ready to do the same today?

Notice this dynamic: The women worship and praise while the men engage the enemy in battle. I want you to note the mention of Barak's father's name. This again emphasizes the importance of legacy and our children contending with what we did not confront.

> In the days of Jael, the roads were abandoned;
>> travelers took to winding paths.
> Village life in Israel ceased,
>> ceased until I, Deborah, arose,
>> arose as a mother in Israel . . .
> From the heavens the stars fought,
>> from their courses they fought against Sisera.
> The river Kishon swept them away,
>> the age-old river, the river Kishon.
>> March on, my soul; be strong! (Judges 5:6–7, 20-21 NIV)

Jael's choice to simply use what was in her hand so distinguished her that they used her name to describe a time period. This woman understood when the enemy comes into your home, you must take him out with whatever means are available.

So, What Is in *Your* Hand?

God will always begin with what is in your hand, even if it seems insignificant. The first time we hear this question, God is talking to Moses, but its wisdom extends to us today. Moses had encountered God in the burning bush, and after relaying his list of reasons he was not the one for the job, God replied with this question:

> *"What is that in your hand?" "A staff,"* he replied.
>
> (Exodus 4:2 NIV)

I have to wonder if Moses was thinking the staff was a rather common object, and a bit unsure how it was going to go over in Pharaoh's court. After all, a staff is really just an upgraded stick, and Moses must have thought there was nothing particularly extraordinary about his. Of course, it is true there is nothing extraordinary about any of us until God begins to anoint what is in our hands. Look at these examples:

- Abigail had her portion of the feast to stay an angry group of men bent on murder.
- Jael had her mallet and tent peg to slay the commander of the enemy's army.
- Samson had his donkey jawbone to slay a thousand men.
- Ruth had grain gleaned from the field.
- Samuel had anointing oil to proclaim a shepherd boy king.
- David had his sling and stones to slay the mighty Philistine champion.
- The unnamed women in the tower under siege had a millstone.
- An unnamed little boy had five loaves and two fishes.
- The broken daughter had an alabaster box filled with oil to anoint Jesus.

Why are we always so busy looking for the out of the ordinary when God is simply asking for what is in our hands? Understand, the common becomes mighty when He anoints it. Offer what He has placed in your hand.

> The common becomes mighty when He anoints it.

"What is in your hand" means whatever is in your care or control. This could be money or possessions. It could be talents and abilities. What you withhold or refuse to give from your hand is often very revealing of what resides within your heart.

Years ago, I came to the realization of what was in my hand. It was the Word God made flesh in my life. My cry for freedom had birthed books that declared His goodness and power. I passed on in each of my books what He had done. In *Out of Control and Loving It!* I shared how He set me free to face my fears so I could be fearless. In *The True Measure of a Woman,* I wrote of how He revealed what was truly of value. In *You Are Not What You Weigh,* I celebrated freedom from an eating disorder. In *Be Angry but Don't Blow It!* I shared how I constructively learned how to navigate anger issues. In *Kissed the Girls and Made Them Cry,* I was able to turn my sexual regret into empowerment for His daughters. I may not have a tent peg, but I have a laptop. With this weapon, I write what I know and share the truth of the gospel's transformation in my life. Why is it important that we know what is in our hands?

> Stretch out your hand to heal and perform miraculous signs and wonders through the name of your holy servant Jesus.
>
> (Acts 4:30 NIV)

How is this accomplished? As we release what is in our hands, He releases what is in His.

———

Heavenly Father,

I come to You in the name of Jesus. Reveal what is in my hand. I want to see Your healing and mighty power to deliver revealed through my life and what I have influence over. Father, begin to anoint the areas of my life where Your Word has been made flesh. Let this expression come through whatever medium You desire. I will write, I will speak, I will sing, I will give, I will create, I will serve, I will steward my life wisely. Awaken the heart of a mother in me. Give me, as You gave Jael, the understanding of the power of the moment. I want to make a difference in my world and in the lives of others. Show me the power of what is in my hand so I will be an answer and never a problem. Anoint it to help me fight with what I possess. Amen.

———

CHAPTER FIFTEEN

The Power of the Moment

Because you have chosen to serve a living God, the concept of the moment or the now is going to be increasingly important for you. I awoke this morning and heard this in my spirit: *Your past and your future intersect in this moment called now.* What does this mean? To me, it speaks of the ultimate importance of weighing our choices and our words.

The choices we make in the now can be driven by the counsel of our past. Perhaps the counsel of fear: *Don't do that . . . last time you failed . . . last time you were hurt . . . don't risk it again.* Or even the counsel of pride: *You're so talented, you don't even need to ask God about this one . . . Everything you do prospers; why seek Him now? It will just slow you down.* Or it could be counsel drawn from God's faithfulness: *He has never failed me. Why should I doubt Him now?*

No matter what your paradigm, there is one thing for certain: The choices we make in the now, whether for good or bad, exert incredible influence on our futures. We can actually make a conscientious choice today to not allow our pasts to dictate our choices, but there is no way we can stop our present choices from affecting our futures. Therefore, seeing we are poised on a threshold of choices, what must we do to seize the moment?

So Many Choices, So Little Time

Now to him who is able to do immeasurably more than all we ask or imagine, according to his power that is at work within us . . . (Ephesians 3:20 NIV)

I have to admit, the word *now* in the above verse really used to frustrate me. I remember when I first became a Christian, every story in the Bible became alive and possible to me. No longer was God distant and uninvolved, watching from a throne high in the sky, expecting me to fail. He was intimately involved with me on a very personal level and cheering me on to victory. As I journeyed through the Old Testament, I saw there was no question of God's presence or involvement with His children Israel. He shook the mountain and accompanied them through the wilderness as a cloud by day and a pillar of fire by night. He fed them manna and quail. His ear was so attentive to them, He even heard the whispers of murmuring and complaining. He heard the gossip and secret questioning of Moses' integrity. If rebellion became an issue, the earth opened up and swallowed the offenders or leprosy broke out and marked them, serving as a warning to others.

And now this same all-encompassing God loved me as His own! I began to invite Him into various areas of my life, and I embraced a position of watchfulness in my daily course of action. As I walked across the campus, I'd pray silently for the people I passed. I would sit alone on campus benches and really wonder if I could cause the mountains to "be removed." Not wanting to be the cause of catastrophe, I would childishly pray for a "slight trembling." I wanted a sign that proved God accepted my prayers and offerings of faith. I fully expected to return to the sorority house and hear that there had been a slight earthquake in the Catalina Mountains. Mind you, I didn't want any property damage; I just thought it would really be helpful if God could show up and show off. (It didn't happen.)

I would pass people in wheelchairs and ask God if I should say to them, "Do you want to be made well?" There arose a dilemma in me each time. I knew and believed God was in fact a healer. The entire counsel of the Bible, from front to back, declares Him as such. But what if nothing happened? Would I reproach His reputation if I raised their hope, only to have it crash head-on with disappointment? Was I the issue? Was there unbelief, a lack of faith or prayer and fasting? I knew God was all-powerful, so His ability was never the issue. As we scan the Old Testament, we see there is no room to question God's power or His awesome wonder.

> *Your right hand, O LORD, was majestic in power. Your right hand, O LORD, shattered the enemy. In the greatness of your majesty you threw down those who opposed you. You unleashed your burning anger; it consumed them like stubble. By the blast of your nostrils the waters piled up. The surging waters stood firm like a wall; the deep waters congealed in the heart of the sea.* (Exodus 15:6–8 NIV)

> *Who among the gods is like you, O LORD? Who is like you— majestic in holiness, awesome in glory, working wonders? You stretched out your right hand and the earth swallowed them. In your unfailing love you will lead the people you have redeemed. In your strength you will guide them to your holy dwelling.* (Exodus 15:11–13 NIV)

There had to be something else, something more. Why was so little of His power evident on a daily basis? I loved what He had done back in Old Testament times, but what about now?

As I looked ahead and glimpsed the future through the window found in the book of Revelation, there was again no question or doubt about who is the Boss, the Victor, and ultimately the One who sits on the throne!

> *After this I heard what sounded like the roar of a great multitude in heaven shouting: "Hallelujah! Salvation and glory and power belong to our God."* (Revelation 19:1 NIV)

This is all great . . . but what about now? Even when He is silent, all creation declares His awesome wonder. Even if all He ever did in my life was save me from the pit, then He is even now worthy of all glory, honor, and power. But my heart cries out in the midst of His goodness to see His power. I want to see His hand stretched forth into our now. I believe God is asking His women to cry out and ask for something more.

> *I believe God is asking His women to cry out and ask for something more.*

Show Me the Power

> *Now to him who is able to do immeasurably more than all we ask or imagine, according to his power that is at work within us.*
> (Ephesians 3:20 NIV)

This is a New Testament declaration of God's divine desire. So where is the "immeasurably more than all we ask or imagine"? We find a glimpse of our answer in the next part of the verse. He is able to do all this "according to his power that is at work within us." He has limited Himself to working through our imperfection and foolishness. If we are content with the status quo and the way things are, then there is no reason to pray as outlined in Ephesians 3:20.

You know what I mean, the prayers that are a bit scary and totally out of the realm of our control. But if we are discontented with what we have now, then we need to cry out for something more.

I want to share with you an example of this dynamic from my own life. Shortly after my book *Kissed the Girls and Made Them Cry* was released, I was sitting on my deck listening to worship music and basking in God's goodness. I had just received another in a series of rather discouraging phone calls and was questioning why I, a woman surrounded by men, had even attempted to write on the subject of sexual purity for girls.

Interestingly enough, I had never been so attacked on all fronts as I was with the release of this message. Friendships had shifted, gossip was flying, and I felt as though I was running in circles, alternately explaining or defending my position, my family, or myself. I was feeling extremely used, misunderstood, misjudged, and misrepresented, and therefore, at that moment on the deck, I was feeling extremely sorry for myself.

I was second-guessing everything, and self-doubt and discouragement began to overwhelm me. I knew I had to regroup if I was going to make it through another day. I desperately wanted to hear an encouraging word from heaven, but instead this question was posed to me: *Lisa, what will you let Me do in your meetings?*

Taken aback and a bit confused I answered, "Lord, You can do whatever You want to do in my meetings."

I heard these words so clearly: *I want to touch and heal My daughters of venereal diseases.*

Well, that was a bit mind-blowing. I'd gone to God for comfort, and God confronted me with the impossible! I foolishly imagined myself on a platform, instructing people to come down front or form prayer lines for specific diseases. Somehow, I knew this just wasn't what He had in mind, so I asked, "Lord, what would that look like?"

You tell them I am present to heal them. Tell them I love them and long to heal and take away their shame. Release My word of healing, and I will do the rest.

Then He gave me this word for them:

Praise the LORD, O my soul; all my inmost being, praise his holy name. Praise the LORD, O my soul, and forget not all his benefits—who forgives all your sins and heals all your diseases, who redeems your life from the pit and crowns you with love and compassion, who satisfies your desires with good things so that your youth is renewed like the eagle's.

(Psalm 103:1–5 NIV)

As I looked at this Scripture passage, I realized it was perfectly fitting for this type of healing. It begins with a command for our inmost being to praise His holy name, then admonishes our souls to praise Him and not forget all His benefits. Not only does our Father God in Christ forgive *all* our sins, but He also longs to heal all our diseases. It is interesting how we have no problem believing there is no sin too great for the mercy of God, but we choke on the issue of healing. We declare His power to forgive freely, but often fail to mention His desire to heal. If we do mention His desire to heal, we tend to limit it to the easy fixes or guiltless infirmities.

In the area of venereal disease the issue of sowing and reaping comes into play, and our reasoning kicks in. On a subconscious level, we mistakenly believe women or young girls with venereal disease are getting what they deserve. But in truth, do any of us really get what we deserve? We all deserve judgment, and instead we are given mercy. If we go with this line of reasoning, none of us should receive anything from God because none of us will ever be worthy.

God is extravagant in His restoration. Not only does He redeem our lives from the pit; He crowns us with His love and compassion, satisfies our desires with good, and renews our youth! How could so much goodness be found in one breath?

He Can't Do It Without Us

Now I am going to share something that is not so good. I hesitated with this promise and did not move it immediately into my now. That day on the deck, Jesus had spoken *personally* to me and shared His desire to heal His daughters in my meetings, and I made it all about me. I was already taking heat, and instead of lifting my eyes from the chaos of the enemy's attack, I remained earthbound and hesitant.

What if He didn't heal them?

Well, what if He did?

I am not proud to tell you this, but it is my earnest prayer that you might learn from my failings, disobedience, and unbelief. Time passed, and convicted by the Holy Spirit that I was in fact resisting the answer to my own prayers, I began to release His word of love and healing in my meetings. The following is but one testimony I have received:

> Lisa,
>
> You prayed for healing of venereal disease for women in the audience—that applied to me. And while I literally felt the power of God move through me and I wanted so badly to accept this healing, my mind kept telling me I wasn't REALLY good enough for one of God's miracles and it wasn't REALLY meant for me. I spent the next two weeks in prayer over this while my heart and mind waged this struggle. I remembered Mary's words that you spoke: "Be it unto me, as is your word." I repeated this over and over until my heart, thru obedience and the love of Jesus, overcame Satan's stronghold. This is the first menstrual cycle I've had in twenty-three years with no herpes outbreak.

For twenty-three years she suffered from monthly painful outbreaks of blisters and shame. I believe God wanted to heal her all along. What if I had remained silent again that day? Would she still be suffering?

Probably. What about you? Who or what is waiting to be released when you speak forth God's Word? You see, it is not about us, but He chooses to do His work through us.

> *How, then, can they call on the one they have not believed in? And how can they believe in the one of whom they have not heard? And how can they hear without someone preaching to them?* (Romans 10:14 NIV)

I know this Scripture is referring to the message of salvation, but don't forget that God is the One who tied forgiveness to healing. Do we stop preaching salvation because not all are saved? Do we cease to call Him Savior? Never! Then we should continue to call Him Healer and Deliverer as well. We saw this dynamic of forgiveness and healing in the life of Jesus. He asked the crowd this question:

> *"For which is easier, to say, 'Your sins are forgiven you,' or to say, 'Arise and walk'? But that you may know that the Son of Man has power on earth to forgive sins"—then He said to the paralytic, "Arise, take up your bed, and go to your house."* (Matthew 9:5–6 NKJV)

Jesus spoke this healing as the Son of man, which is key for us. If He had spoken this as the Son of God, we would have room to doubt our involvement in this type of outreach.

Every Christian agrees it is our right and privilege to forgive others as well as to declare God's forgiveness of sin. Correct? None of us doubt we have been entrusted with the ministry of reconciliation. Jesus said, "Which is easier?" meaning, "It is all the same to Me!" He can have them both!

As daughters of God, we have the privilege of not only sharing Jesus' power to forgive with others, we must share as well His power to heal.

Understand that not everyone who hears of God's power to forgive is willing to receive His forgiveness, but we still share the gospel. Healing should be no different.

It's Time!

When the wine was gone, Jesus' mother said to him, "They have no more wine." "Dear woman, why do you involve me?" Jesus replied. "My time has not yet come." His mother said to the servants, "Do whatever he tells you." (John 2:3-5 NIV)

It's a good thing God never considered me for the position of Jesus' mother. I would have done it all wrong. Think about it . . . Jesus was probably around thirty years of age when the wine ran out at the wedding. I probably would have put my hands on my hips and yelled, "Jesus, it's been thirty years of scandal and questions! Now my friends are out of wine. Can You help us out here?! If now is not the time, when will be Your time? I'm Your mother; and son, I'm tired of waiting . . . It's time!"

But Mary didn't do that. She just turned to the servants in attendance at the wedding and said, "Do whatever he tells you," and left it there.

Why was she so confident? It could be because when a mother says it's time . . . it's time.

> When a mother says it's time . . . it's time.

I don't believe I really even understood timing until I became a mother. Before giving birth to my first son, I was under the mistaken impression I had some sort of control over the dynamic of time. I examined my June calendar and picked a few convenient dates for his birth and offered them up as prayer options: "God, I really need to have the baby after this, but no later than this."

I felt the latter part of the week would be best because then my husband would be available to help out over the weekend. But something went amiss; the dates I'd chosen flew past and left me still large and pregnant in their wake.

I was overdue and on the verge of exploding. Stretch marks (which I initially mistook for worms) appeared as my body contorted in an attempt to hold the ever-growing baby and my ribs in place. I was getting a bit testy as well. Comments like, "Are you still pregnant?" which a week earlier would have received a smile and an explanation, were now met with open hostility. John winced as he kept me from interpersonal contact with the unaware. I was a time bomb ready go off.

Finally, at two weeks past my due date, the doctor declared me worthy of an induction. I was set to go the next morning. I showed up in full makeup, freshly manicured, and accessorized with jewelry. I obviously had no idea what was in store. Friends have looked at my pictures from the hospital and just laughed. After twelve hours of Pitocin-induced labor, I was a wreck. I'd had my baby, but I started hemorrhaging and was bedridden for two weeks.

When I had my second son, it was a different story. I didn't know I was in labor until almost the end because I was waiting for contractions of the intensity I'd experienced while on Pitocin. I barely made it to the hospital. When I burst onto the scene at Labor and Delivery, I was desperate. I checked in and explained my urgent need. I was informed all the examining rooms were full. To which I replied, "I don't need to be examined . . . I need to be delivered!"

The intensity of my words caused the nurse to look up from my admission papers. "Is this your first baby?"

"No—it's my second!"

With this revelation, everything changed. Everyone began to scurry into action. Why? Because when a mother says it's time . . . it's time.

It's Your Time, Not Your Turn

Through having my babies I learned this valuable lesson: Mothers are not in control of time, but they do recognize when it is time. The phrase "It's your time!" has been stirring in my spirit. Notice I did not say "It's your turn." When it's someone's *turn,* everyone else has to take a break and watch while they take center stage; but when it's *time,* everyone joins in!

Too often when God begins to stir His people and we realize He is preparing to do something awesome, we foolishly begin to jockey for position like the disciples of Jesus. He announced it was His time, and all they wanted to know was who was most important. In their struggle for position, they missed His point and scattered when it was time to take their places.

With more than twenty years of ministry experience, I have had plenty of opportunity to see the "It's my turn" dynamic played out. I've heard men say, "Women, sit down. It's not your turn!" I've heard the women argue back, "Men, sit down. It's our turn now!" I've seen the young shake their heads at the old and say, "You guys are just not getting it! We can't wait until it's our turn." I've heard the older generation tell the young, "It's not your turn yet. Sit back down!" We constantly confuse the term *turn* with *time,* but in the last days this will not be so.

> In the last days, God says, I will pour out my Spirit on all people. Your sons and daughters will prophesy, your young men will see visions, your old men will dream dreams.
>
> (Acts 2:17 NIV)

In the last days everyone's included, for they know it's time for all people. The sons and daughters prophesy and the young see visions and the old dream dreams.

As I have traveled, God has led me to declare repeatedly, "It's time!" But what is it time for? To find our answer, let's revisit the wedding.

It's time for us to be honest and say we are out of wine. It is time to stop calling water wine and settling for quenched thirst when God wants us to have so much more. It is time for us to embrace the One with power to turn water into wine rather than arguing with one another about why the wine is gone. It is time to leave behind the theological debate over whether God can turn our water into His wine. We need to involve Him by simply being honest: "Jesus, we are out of wine." Then just get everything ready. The servants need to be told, "Whatever He tells you to do, do it."

I believe Jesus loves it when we come to the end of this earth's refreshing and ask for His. It is time for the promise of Ephesians 3:20 to become real.

Let's watch Jesus at the wedding:

> *Nearby stood six stone water jars, the kind used by the Jews for ceremonial washing, each holding from twenty to thirty gallons.*
>
> *Jesus said to the servants, "Fill the jars with water"; so they filled them to the brim. Then he told them, "Now draw some out and take it to the master of the banquet." They did so, and the master of the banquet tasted the water that had been turned into wine ... Then he called the bridegroom aside and said, "Everyone brings out the choice wine first and then the cheaper wine after the guests have had too much to drink; but you have saved the best till now." This, the first of his miraculous signs, Jesus performed at Cana in Galilee. He thus revealed his glory, and his disciples put their faith in him.*
>
> (John 2:6–11 NIV, emphasis added)

Can you really believe God has saved the best until now? I know it is often hard to think that way with all we have around us, but I have chosen to continue to cry out for more than what we've seen ... How about you? Women are intimately connected with God in this issue of timing. Could it be God is stirring us to ask for something more? Jesus, what about now?

———

Heavenly Father,

I do believe You have saved the best for now, and I want to be a part of that. I desperately need Your involvement in every area of my life. I am tired of drinking water and calling it wine. I am tired of going to be delivered and instead being only examined. Forgive me for being frightened and drawing back from Your promises. Give me now the gift of faith to believe and receive You as a healer. I am sorry I have been waiting for someone to tell me it was my turn, when all along You have been whispering, "It is time." Anoint me now with Your Word and Your promises. Amen.

———

CHAPTER SIXTEEN

You Are Being Watched!

There is something somewhat unnerving about knowing you are being watched. Though none of us imagine we can consistently escape the watchful eyes of others, we often live unaware that our lives are on display on a much grander scale than even the most paranoid human could imagine. I can't even count the number of times I have been bouncing and singing at stoplights, only to look over and catch the amusement on the faces of the drivers beside me. But I am not referring to the casual audience of fellow drivers. There is a much larger and purposeful gathering watching both you and me.

There are times when we know beyond a shadow of a doubt we are not only being watched, but we are on display and possibly being scored or judged. Perhaps we have found ourselves in a similar dynamic courtesy of a performance or an athletic competition of which we chose to be part. Maybe we were in this position in a speech class or when giving a business presentation. The eyes of judges, teachers, or potential clients were upon us, watching. They sat there, arms crossed, daring us to impress them. To get the A, the job, or win the award, we had to do *something* unique that caused us to stand out and earn the label of exceptional or outstanding among our peers.

Honestly, this was a situation I hated above all others. At swimming meets I would melt down at the mere announcement of my event: "Fifty-yard butterfly, report to the blocks." I would run to the bathroom, overwhelmed by nerves. I didn't want to win; I just wanted the race to be over. If I was to give a speech, I became so nervous I lost all composure, remembrance of content, and concentration. As far as performances, I rarely signed up to be part of anything that could potentially position me front and center. I was afraid of any audience that numbered more than two.

The truth is, even now I have a hard time navigating situations where I sense competition. My husband, John, is unfazed by this tension, but if I am in a gathering where people begin to position themselves for power, I prefer to let them know I'm no threat, by bowing out and in essence saying, "How about I just say, 'You win'?"

There is another uncomfortable type of critical, watchful situation. This one is not about competition or performance, because you have already lost before you've begun. This tension is found in an environment where you are already deemed guilty or lacking. More often than not, we do not disappoint those who expect our failure.

Watching for Someone to Fail—or Win

Enough of the negative aspects of watchfulness. There's a positive side to being watched. There is the excitement of being watched because you've "got it going on." I love watching my boys at sporting events. I will repeatedly yell "You're the man!" My children will either act mildly annoyed or pretend they don't know or hear me, which only makes me yell louder. At the end of the game, they will congratulate the other players and shyly begin to reconnect with their embarrassing mother, but in the car it all changes. "Did you see me make that goal?" "Did you see that pass?" They are so excited, and they want to be sure I didn't miss any of it.

At other times, John or I may be in the middle of something when we are interrupted by one of our boys as they cry out for our attention from their trampoline: "Watch me land this flip!" They'll invite us out for a group celebration of what they have already mastered in private. When they were younger, we would hear them excitedly call to us when they had completed some Lego masterpiece, actually cleaned their room well, or finished some arduous school project.

"Mom, Dad, look at this!" It was a cry filled with triumph and unabashed joy in their accomplishment. We'd laugh and clap our hands or otherwise encourage them. All the while sharing in their excitement, knowing they had broken through another barrier into a new level of confidence. The more we cheered, the more they wanted to show off. If we were negligent to make the connection and celebrate these small victories with them, their voices would fade and we would discover them celebrating their victories in solitude. If we failed to encourage them or criticized the attempts they presented, it was as though they shrank in disappointment before our eyes. There is definitely a difference between being expected to fail and being expected to win.

One of my children is particularly sensitive to this type of interaction. With him, I have seen more success with the approach of "I'll be back to check your room in fifteen minutes, and I know you will do a great job!" than I do with "I'll be up in fifteen minutes, and you better have this done!" One lends creativity and reward to an atmosphere of obedience, while the other threatens discipline and consequence. I confess that I am wired this way as well. I am capable of a complete shutdown if there is no expectation of hope for my success in those watching me. But there is so much more than hope found in the watching we all are experiencing. There is awe and wonder.

Everything God made is waiting with excitement for God to show his children's glory completely. Everything God made

> *was changed to become useless, not by its own wish but be-*
> *cause God wanted it and because all along there was this*
> *hope: that everything God made would be set free from ruin*
> *to have the freedom and glory that belong to God's children.*
>
> (Romans 8:19–21 NCV)

This is watching of a very different kind. This time, it is not just people, but everything is watching us—even things we didn't know had eyes are waiting excitedly for this show of freedom and glory reserved to be revealed through God's beloved children. We are not being weighed under the critical scrutiny of creation or on some terrestrial stage as every living thing and

> *The audience surrounding us is filled with joyful expectation.*

earthly element challenges us to impress them with our human actions and stuff. We are not involved in some sort of competition where only the best contestant wins. Nor is there an atmosphere of exhausted impatience . . . The audience surrounding us is filled with joyful expectation.

Imagine the strength and joy that could be imparted to each of us if we would only realize this truth! We are enveloped with the enthusiasm of the earth and all its fullness as it gazes upon us with an attitude of expectant anticipation.

Creation is not even concerned with the possibility of our failure. We've already done that. As the descendants and seeds of Adam, we were present and accounted for in him when creation was changed and subjected to this domain of useless ruin. I have to wonder if creation gasped in horror at our reckless boldness when the woman and the man grasped at equality with God, ignoring His one directive.

Did creation shiver as death's cold shadow began to stretch itself over the warmth of the garden? Were there tears as the man and the woman were banished from God's presence? Did the plants rustle among themselves as they watched and wondered what would happen now that those who guarded and kept them were cast out and separated from their abundance? Did the trees shudder as Adam and Eve hid among them? Did their branches break for the first time as the man and the woman pushed past them as they left the garden? Did the grass bend under their feet, only to discover it no longer sprang immediately upright? How long did the process of death and destruction take before its effect was known on creation? Was it so gradual that it was centuries before the Fall was apparent?

We know the Fall's destructive effects were felt immediately by the man and the woman. As Adam and Eve left the garden they were shadowed by darkness, shame, and death. They watched helplessly as fighting, betrayal, jealousy, and murder gained entrance and overtook the lives of their children. Adam's and Eve's choices affected everything. Even though they lived for several hundred years after the Fall, the reign of death had begun.

Our Trespass Versus His Gift

Nevertheless, death reigned from the time of Adam to the time of Moses, even over those who did not sin by breaking a command, as did Adam, who was a pattern of the one to come. But the gift is not like the trespass. *For if the many died by the trespass of the one man, how much more did God's grace and the gift that came by the grace of the one man, Jesus Christ, overflow to the many!* (Romans 5:14–15 NIV, emphasis added)

When Jesus chose to lay down His life, everything was reversed and it all began to change again. Just as it took awhile for both creation and mankind to manifest the tangible effects of death, even though they were set immediately into motion, so it is with us. For two thousand years death has been losing its grip, and sooner than we know, it will all change. I love this truth: "But the gift is not like the trespass." The trespass of one brought death to many, but know this: His gift is always more powerful than our trespasses.

Again, the gift of God is not like the result of the one man's
sin: The judgment followed one sin and brought condemna-
tion, but the gift followed many trespasses and brought justi-
fication. For if, by the trespass of the one man, death reigned
through that one man, how much more will those who re-
ceive God's abundant provision of grace and of the gift of
righteousness reign in life through the one man, Jesus Christ.
(Romans 5:16–17 NIV)

We no longer live under the transgression of Adam but under the
righteous reign of Jesus Christ. Creation no longer looks upon us with
scorn and questioning. Creation looks on us with hope and with the understanding that the finality of death's reign is over. The old order has
passed away, and the promise of the new stretches before us.

For what is seen is temporary, but what is unseen is eternal.
(2 Corinthians 4:18 NIV)

Death may reign in the realm of the seen, but Jesus reigns in the realm
of the eternal. We have truly been freed and justified, even though the total
restoration is not yet realized. Could it be that time itself was created to
highlight this journey? Regardless, the end of time as we know it is quickly
approaching. The great exchange will take place and then the visible will
be overtaken by the invisible, the mortal will be replaced by the immortal,
and death itself will be swallowed up in victory. Before all of creation, the
shame of man will be displaced by God's glory, and we will be lifted into
heavenly places to be with Him. When this release happens, we will com-
prehend what the glorious revelation and transforming truth of being "in
Christ" actually looks like. Then and only then will man, woman, the creatures, and all of creation be restored to its original freedom and glory.

Therefore we do not lose heart. Though outwardly we are
wasting away, yet inwardly we are being renewed day by day.

For our light and momentary troubles are achieving for us an
eternal glory that far outweighs them all. So we fix our eyes
not on what is seen, but on what is unseen. For what is seen
is temporary, but what is unseen is eternal.

(2 Corinthians 4:16–18 NIV)

Even now, creation holds its breath in joyous expectancy of our utter and complete victory in Him. All creation cries out to us in its unique voice: "Sons of Adam and Daughters of Eve, have you forgotten what He's done? Don't you know the price that was paid? You are no longer guardians of shame; you are the children of God. Don't look at what is. Don't you see what He is about to do?" Everywhere we look, creation issues its wondrous and insistent invitation: "Sons and Daughters of Adam and Eve, stop living for what perishes and frustrates. Stop looking at what you now see . . . There is more!"

Creation understands something we have lost sight of: There is no longer any possibility of failure, because it is not about us . . . it is about Him.

We Must Speak God's Language

It is written: "I believed; therefore I have spoken." With that same spirit
of faith we also believe and therefore speak, because we know that the one
who raised the Lord Jesus from the dead will also raise us with Jesus and
present us with you in his presence. (2 Corinthians 4:13–14 NIV)

We must again receive the spirit of faith that speaks for the unseen and yet unrealized, rather than the current very real death and destruction. As children of God, we must speak His language of hope and power.

Now faith is the substance of things hoped for, the evidence
of things not seen. (Hebrews 11:1 NKJV)

Notice how the words *now* and *faith* are connected as evidence and assurance of what yet remains unseen in this temporary realm of the seen and heard.

I have often heard this question posed in one form or another: What would you do or attempt or dream if you knew you could not fail? This is an amazing, thought-provoking question, one that challenges us to override the limits in our thinking. But even with all our imagining, there remains a hitch: Humans fail. This truth is glaringly apparent for all to see and constantly repeated in history. But redemption is God's answer to mankind's failure.

We may invite those around to watch us if we are certain we will not fail, but whom do we invite to watch us when we are certain we will? God is not asking what we would venture if we could not fail. Adam and Eve took the fruit in secret, thinking it would ensure them complete success. God is not going down that road again; there is no secret garden this time. He is preparing to blow our minds and do what only One who cannot fail can accomplish. This is the reason God has encouraged all creation to watch what's about to happen. The Fall happened privately in a garden, but the extreme makeover will happen in the sight of all. All of creation and every creature will be made completely new, not just tweaked and nipped and tucked, but totally transformed. Even the heavens will be replaced as the old passes away.

> *Then I saw a new heaven and a new earth, for the first heaven and the first earth had passed away, and there was no longer any sea.*   (Revelation 21:1 NIV)

From the very beginning, as man accelerated toward destruction, God had a plan to make all things new. In the book of Revelation alone He declares this awesome truth four times.

> *"I am the Alpha and the Omega," says the Lord God, "who is, and who was, and who is to come, the Almighty."*
>
>   (Revelation 1:8 NIV)

The end of the story has never been in question. It has never been about us or our accomplishments . . . it has always been about Him. As sons and daughters of Adam, we look at the world around us or at ourselves and cannot fathom a life that has never known failure, a life that is almighty and without flaw or weakness. A life without beginning or end puts our human mind on "tilt." One who has the answer before there is even a question defies all our natural human reason. The One without match or equal is the very One who will completely transform us to reveal His glory.

> *The sufferings we have now are nothing compared to the great glory that will be shown to us.* (Romans 8:18 NCV)

Creation is not watching us, arms crossed, challenging us to impress them. Actually, they are nodding their approval and lifting their voices in unison, saying, "You go, girl! Fight fearlessly the battle only you can win, and wield with strength again the weapons God entrusted to your care. You are the very one we have been watching for. Be empowered to . . .":

Cover others with love.
Raise them with honor.
Empower them with wisdom.
Encourage them with vision.
Restore their dreams with purity.
Recover their strength with joy.
Free them with His truth.
Give them a future with legacy.
Awe them with beauty.
Inspire them with His splendor.
Stir them with holiness and passion.

The Towel Cape

I want to leave you with this mixture of images from my childhood and hope for the future. I'm in a dream filled with sunshine, laughter, and childhood memories. Dressed only in cut-off shorts, I run with bare chest and feet through the warmth of a summer long gone. Behind me trails my source of power. A cape. It propelled me down the sun-dappled winding trails of the ravine and pushed me to the limits of earthly speed barriers as I raced down the straightaway of white-hot sidewalks.

In actuality, the cape was a small bath or hand towel pinned together at my throat by the mother of one of the boys I was playing with. If I ran fast enough, it soared behind me as I navigated turns. For some reason I didn't want it touching my back until I stopped. Perhaps I feared this meant losing a portion of its power. For every child knows, capes truly empower only as they sail behind you. Without the wind lifting them, they are but agents of coverage.

I awake with a smile as the daylight pulls me gently from my dream. I vividly remember the cape and the boys. I also remember the day I was told I no longer could be part of their group of caped crusaders. Why? It was simply that I was a girl.

It was hot out, and I'd removed my sweaty shirt in preparation for the adorning of the towel. I stood straight and tall beside my best friends, Phil and Stuart, when a question was raised by a mother. Wasn't I a bit old to be removing my shirt?

Mind you, I'm certain I was under the age of seven, and all of our chests looked exactly the same. I was a bit confused. She suggested I put my shirt back on. I looked down at my sweaty cast-off shirt, flung like a tent on the deep summer grass. Last summer had been different . . . There had been no questions asked as we all three embraced the ritual of disrobing with wild, almost tribal, abandon.

I was conflicted. Yes, it was true I was a girl, but I was *not* a girly girl. I wasn't afraid of leeches or ticks, and I plunged into muddy creeks without hesitation. I accepted all dares and endured outings to the mummy's mansion (a concrete bunker we imagined an ancient Egyptian tomb) fearlessly. How could my merit of the towel be in question? Wasn't I at that moment outside rather than in the cool comfort of air-conditioning, playing with some Barbie? It wasn't right!

Somehow, I knew if I put the shirt on, I'd never be able to take it off again.

Sensing my hesitation, that mother suggested I wear the cape over my shirt. We three exchanged doubtful glances. It just would not be the same, and we all knew it.

How would I feel the warmth of the sun? The wind? The power?

Dejected, but feeling I had no other choice, I put on the shirt.

After this first alteration of wardrobe, my role in the threesome was seriously impacted. I was no longer offered the choice role of Superman, Batman, or Robin. The only one I was offered was Cat Woman because, after all, it had become glaringly apparent that I was in fact . . . a girl.

I no longer ran with the boys; they ran *from* me.

From Caped Crusader to Cat Woman

Without ever meaning to, I had switched sides and was now an enemy. Apparently Cat Woman's goal was to trap good guys and scratch them. As they ran away, I protested vehemently, "Come back, come back! I'm not going to scratch you!"

But they wouldn't hear of it. The die had been cast and my options reduced. It was either play with Barbies or play Cat Woman.

Oh, even back then I felt limited by the roles offered. How many of you were aware there must be something more? Do you understand that the world too frequently sorts itself into the camps of Boy Toys or Man Scratchers? (Really talented women may even end up being both.)

Actually, the only real possibility or source for something authentically more and different is the Christian woman. The Daughters of Promise, Sarah's fearless seed, the very ones who are awakening the world over and arising in their quest for more. These mothers in Israel and sisters of fire, young and old, are shaking free of the images and foolishness bombarding and limiting them, and lifting their eyes. They have glimpsed the city at dawn and know they will be free only where truth reigns supreme. Like you, they are hungry for something more than what they've seen. They are willing to pay the price to leave behind this world's nightmare and enter a dream.

As I write, one of my sons has surprised me by coming in through the door, rosy-cheeked from the blustery fall day. He has a cape on. His is a bit larger than mine ever was; his cape is a twin-sized flannel sheet tied around his neck. He has been jumping on the trampoline and felt the wind as it lifted his cape like a sail. In his excitement he has bounded in to show me his adornment. It makes me smile . . . Yes, it is time to fashion something in our lives that can catch the wind of the spirit so that we might be propelled farther than any strength that is our own.

He spread his cape out to full arm's-length span, like an eagle stretching its wings, and said, "Mom, I am blocking the light from the window so you can write!"

Smiling, I thank him. He shares the hope that his brother will join him soon in his wind chase when he comes home from school. A typical mother, I default to the suggestion that what they really need to do is clean their room, which I found so frightening earlier in the day.

Undaunted by my suggestion, he answers back enthusiastically, "But Mommy, the wind won't last!"

Oh, the simple truths of childhood—to know and understand that there will always be messy rooms . . . but the wind won't last. Even now he waits at the back door for his brother, sheet in hand.

Spread Your Cape

And for you there blows a wind as well. It is always captured in the moment. Spread your cape and recapture a portion of what has been stolen by your enemy the serpent. He hates it that you have found out

God wants you to connect to a source so far from earthly limitations and confines.

The brother is home, and even now my boys are laughing, jumping, and toppling each other on the trampoline. Their capes are so large they are being entangled in them. They are so much grander than the puny little towel I imagined caused me to fly. Their billowing sheets are more than tenfold its size and threaten to totally engulf them as they leap heavenward, alternately laughing and screaming. But isn't that just the way it should be?

Each generation should walk in abundantly more freedom than the one before it. We must enlarge our sails and allow the wind of His Spirit more square footage to harness what God wants to do with each passing generation.

It is my earnest prayer that you will turn your eyes toward just such a hope. Perhaps there is now but a washcloth tucked into the back of your collar. Allow the Holy Spirit to exchange this small square of terry cloth for something bigger. I think a diaphanous flowing cape is in order. Allow the Holy Spirit to remove every drape of shame and cover you with another one more outfitted to who you will be.

The unveiling is at hand. A new mystery and longing is present in the daughters of the Most High. A voice has whispered to me for years, urging me onward in prayer:

> *Cry out for the unveiling of My daughter. She must be revealed, released, and freed to both respond and be responded to.*

In my mind's eye I again see the upright pillar of stone wrapped in layers of fabric. Each year another sheet comes off and a bit more of the form is revealed. At first the outer drapes were like a painter's tarp, but with each peeling away the fabric has become more fluid and beautiful. Even now I can see contours of the form once so distorted a few years ago. I look and know without a doubt she will be beautiful. I catch in her frame the glimpse of you. Do you see it? Let the unveiling begin.

Heavenly Father,

I come before You in the most precious name of Jesus. I ask for the counsel and wisdom of Your Holy Spirit to enlighten me as I pray.

Father, I do believe You created me as an answer and not a problem. I receive the unique privilege and honor that accompany my feminine nature. Anoint me not only to fight the battles I have been uniquely called to fight, but show me what that looks like as a woman. I want to be the daughter this world is watching and waiting for. I want to release wisdom and truth in my world and sphere of influence. I want to raise and bestow honor as only a woman can. I want to fight with what is in my hand. I want to see the cordial of healing poured forth.

Unveil Your purpose for me as a daughter of God. Release me from any and every chain or bondage. Call me altogether lovely, and I will listen. I am ready to be a woman who truly fights like a girl—with wisdom, strength, and honor. Let the light of Your Word dispel any and all darkness that would tempt me to depart from the path of life and displace men or grasp at equality with God. I celebrate my unique and valuable portion and part. May Your kingdom come and Your will be done in my earth as it is in heaven. Amen.

Notes

Chapter One: You Fight Like a Girl!
1. *New Unger's Bible Dictionary,* s.v. *enmity.*

Chapter Three: But I Am Not a Man
1. J. R. R. Tolkien, *The Return of the King* New York: Houghton Mifflin: 2nd Reprint edition (March 1, 1988).

Chapter Four: Finding Center
1. *Webster's Encyclopedic Unabridged Dictionary of the English Language,* s.v. *male.*
2. Ibid., s.v. *female.*
3. Ibid., s.v. *nuclei.*
4. Ibid., s.v. *feminine.*
5. Ibid., s.v. *woman.*
6. Ibid., s.v. *grace.*

Chapter Six: When Do Women Strike?
1. C. S. Lewis, *The Lion, the Witch and the Wardrobe* New York: Harper Collins; Reprint edition (July 8, 1994).
2. Ibid.
3. Ibid.

united states
PO BOX 888
PALMER LAKE, CO 80133-0888

800.648.1477 *us and canada
T:719.487.3000
F:719.487.3300

mail@MessengerInternational.org

For **more** information
please contact us:

Messenger
International®

life-transforming truth.

europe
PO BOX 622
NEWPORT, NP19 8ZJ
UNITED KINGDOM

44(0) 870.745.5790
F:44(0) 870.745.5791

europe@MessengerInternational.org

WOMEN:
Join Lisa Bevere's **ENGAGE** program.
Visit us online at
www.MessengerInternational.org

australia
PO BOX 6200
DURAL, D.C. NSW 2158
AUSTRALIA

IN AUS: 1.300.650.577
+61.2.8850.1725
F:+61 2.8850.1735

aus@MessengerInternational.org

Books by Lisa

Be Angry, But Don't Blow It!
Fight Like a Girl
Kissed the Girls and Made Them Cry
Nurture
Out of Control and Loving It!
The True Measure of a Woman
You Are Not What You Weigh

Fight Like *a Girl*
The Power of Being a Woman

Curriculum Includes

12 Sessions on 4 DVD's
Hardback Book and Interactive Workbook
Makeup Bag
Bracelet

Why is it that women often don't like women? What could possibly cause a large portion of us to reject our own gender? More often than not we lack and appreciation for women. We associate men with strength and women with weakness. We therefore attempt life in roles as men, only to find ourselves conflicted. But God is awakening and empowering His daughters to realize who they truly are, as well as their unique and significant contributions.

bringing healing to women of all ages.

KISSED THE GIRLS AND MADE THEM CRY

CURRICULUM INCLUDES

12 SESSIONS ON 3 DVD'S, BOOK,
INTERACTIVE WORKBOOK, MAKEUP BAG
BONUS Q&A DVD

Don't believe the lie—sexual purity isn't about rules...it's about freedom and power. It is time to take back what we've cheaply given away. The *Kissed the Girls and Made Them Cry* kit is not only designed for youth but also for women of all ages who long for a greater intimacy with Jesus and need to embrace God's healing and restoring love.

"I'm 15. and through your kit my nightmare has been turned back to a dream!"

additional RESOURCES

Beautiful -DVD

Part of being beautiful and authentic is realizing the value of you, the original! An original is the beginning of something. You were never meant to be defined by others and reduced to a pseudo copy or forgery. Do you know there is something extremely unique and beautiful only you have? Whether you embrace your uniqueness or live out your life as only a mixed blend of the lives of others is really up to you. But know this - the whole world is watching in the hope that you will be a beautiful original.

Life Without Limits -DVD

It is definitely no longer about us, but about Him! God is calling a generation of women who are willing to take risks and go out over their heads in Him. Women brave enough to trust Him with every area of their life. He is watching for wild women who will be reckless in both their abandonment to God and their commitment to obedience. It is time to embrace His freedom in every area. This powerful and dynamic video was recorded at a women's mentoring conference and will empower you in these crucial areas:
- Completing versus competing
- Making your marriage a place of power
- Refining and defining your motivation
- Harnessing your power of influence
- Answering the mandate

Extreme Makeover -2 CD SET

Makeovers of every kind are the current craze. Not only are faces and bodies being hauled over, but everything is subject to this before-and-after experimentation. People just can't seem to get enough, and rather than judging, the church needs to ask the all-important question…Why? I believe it is because we are all desperate for change!

It's Time -CD

For too long we have had the attitude, "It's my turn!" But when God begins to pour out His spirit, it is nobody's turn, it becomes everybody's time. It is time for God's gifts in His body to come forth. The Father is gifting men and women alike to shine in each and every realm of life. Discover what He has placed in your hand and join the dance of a lifetime.